TROPICAL TONGUES

STUDIES IN LATIN AMERICA

The Studies in Latin America series features short works published by the Institute for the Study of the Americas at the University of North Carolina at Chapel Hill. Print editions are distributed by UNC Press, and the University of North Carolina at Chapel Hill Library hosts open access digital editions. The series promotes new scholarship on Latin America and the Caribbean focusing on the social sciences—principally anthropology, geography, history, political science, and sociology—and featuring diverse methodological approaches and perspectives on vital issues concerning Latin America and the Caribbean, past and present. For more information visit http://isa.unc.edu/programs-activities/studies/in/latin/america/.

TROPICAL TONGUES

*Language Ideologies, Endangerment,
and Minority Languages in Belize*

Jennifer Carolina Gómez Menjívar
and William Noel Salmon

INSTITUTE FOR THE STUDY OF THE AMERICAS
AT THE UNIVERSITY OF NORTH CAROLINA AT CHAPEL HILL

INSTITUTE **FOR THE** STUDY OF THE AMERICAS

This book was generously supported by funding from the UNC Press Thomas W. Ross Fund and from the Office of the Dean of the College of Arts and Sciences at the University of North Carolina at Chapel Hill.

Suggested citation: Gómez Menjívar, Jennifer Carolina, and William Noel Salmon. *Tropical Tongues: Language Ideologies, Endangerment, and Minority Languages in Belize.* Chapel Hill: Institute for the Study of the Americas at the University of North Carolina at Chapel Hill, 2018.
doi: https://doi.org/10.5149/9781469641416_GomezMenjivar

Library of Congress Cataloging-in-Publication Data
Names: Gómez Menjívar, Jennifer Carolina, author. | Salmon, William Noel, author.
Title: Tropical tongues : language ideologies, endangerment, and minority languages in Belize / Jennifer Carolina Gómez Menjívar and William Noel Salmon.
Other titles: Studies in Latin America.
Description: Chapel Hill : Institute for the Study of the Americas at the University of North Carolina at Chapel Hill, [2018] | Series: Studies in Latin America | Includes bibliographical references.
Identifiers: LCCN 2017046221 | ISBN 9781469641393 (pbk : alk. paper)
Subjects: LCSH: Languages in contact—Belize. | Belize—Languages. | Creole dialects, English—Belize. | Mopan dialect—Belize. | Garifuna language—Belize.
Classification: LCC P40.5.L382 B424 2018 | DDC 306.44/97282—dc23
LC record available at https://lccn.loc.gov/2017046221

ISBN 978-1-4696-4139-3 (pbk: alk. paper)
ISBN 978-1-4696-4141-6 (ebook)

Published by the Instutute for the Study of the Americas
at the University of North Carolina at Chapel Hill

Distributed by the University of North Carolina Press
www.uncpress.org

For our boys

Contents

Tables and Maps

Preface

Tropical Tongues examines the precarious state of minority languages in coastal Belize as Kriol (a minority language) has risen to the level of a "national language" in the period following the country's independence (1981–present). Our research shows that while the overt prestige enjoyed by English and Spanish is indisputable, the linguistic ecology of Kriol gives it a covert prestige among women and the young people who reside in the districts along the coast. Our data include ethnographic observation, ethnographic interviews, language attitude surveys, and language use surveys that together take the pulse of Kriol as well as the place and future of other minority languages in the country. The chapters in this book are written with attention to the varying degrees of prestige and stigmatization that the minority languages we study have acquired over the last thirty-six years.

The introduction to this work situates our research within the larger context of minority languages in Latin America. We examine the shifting positions of minority languages from the colonial period forward in the contexts today known as Nicaragua, Guatemala, Mexico, and Paraguay. That indigenous languages become endangered and often disappear is universally known; but to date, there is little discussion about how the rise of a minority language relates to language shift among coexisting minority languages in this region.

Chapter 1 provides historical, geographic, and linguistic background on the many languages in contact in Belize. It also provides an account of our methodology, from our mixed-methods research design to the analysis of survey and ethnographic data we collected.

Chapter 2 focuses on Kriol, and its rise from a subaltern language to the national language of Belize. We report findings from a verbal guise test with 141 participants of different ethnic backgrounds in Belize City and Punta Gorda and examine these quantitative data together with qualitative data on language attitudes. The discussion here focuses on the informal/formal settings and national/foreign contexts that speakers of Kriol in Belize City and Punta Gorda attribute to the varieties of Kriol spoken in their hometowns.

Chapter 3 focuses on Mopan, one of the three Mayan languages spoken in Belize. We report on the results of language surveys administered to seventy-eight participants in a Mopan village of approximately 800 inhabitants. Our findings in this chapter uncover a linguistic hierarchy in which the prestige attributed to Kriol varies by the Mopan participant's sex and age. Our discussion covers the socioeconomic transitions experienced by Mayan communities in the country and the disparate effects of these changes on Mayan elders and their descendants.

Chapter 4 addresses Garifuna, an Afro-indigenous language spoken in Belize, Honduras, Guatemala, and Nicaragua. We surveyed fifty participants on Garifuna language use and collected ethnographic data in eleven locations throughout the villages of Seine Bight and Placencia. Our findings in this chapter show that Garifuna language use is extremely limited. We discuss the deep regret expressed by elders over language loss, the younger generation's lack of interest in its recovery, and the almost mythical Belizean village that all our participants spoke about with *saudade* as the last stronghold of the Garifuna language.

We conclude with a discussion of the forces of change on the languages spoken on the Caribbean coast of Belize—English, Spanish, Kriol, Garifuna, and Mopan—with special attention to the growing tourist industry and its far-reaching effects on the coastal cultures and languages. In addition to addressing pride and prestige in local languages, we give an account of the shifting gender dynamics, widened generation gaps, changes in religious and educational institutions, employment opportunities in tourist hubs, the decline of local fishing industries, and the "integration" of hitherto isolated geographic areas into the national fold—all of which contribute to the interactions between the languages spoken on the Belizean coast.

Tropical Tongues has developed over the course of four years of fieldwork in coastal Belize. It contributes to a much-needed body of research on language ecologies, language attitudes, and language use in Latin America. We believe that this study can serve as a blueprint for understanding linguistic hierarchies and language endangerment in plurilingual contexts, whether in Latin America or elsewhere. The interdisciplinary nature of this research, its attention to ethnic and linguistic diversity, and the mixed-methods approach used herein, are put forward in an effort to involve scholars from a wide range of fields in this vital and urgent conversation.

Acknowledgments

We are grateful to many people who have assisted us during the course of our fieldwork. This project would not have been possible without our participants in Belize who generously gave their time in answering our many questions. Special thanks to Ms. Leela Vernon and our colleagues in Belize—Yvette Herrera, Anthony Brown, Ubaldimir Guerra, Gillian Flowers, Tracey Sangster, and Silvaana Udz—for invaluable discussions of the language, culture, and history of Belize. Thanks also to Donald Winford at The Ohio State University, to Nigel Encalada at the National Institute of Culture and History in Belize City, and to James Garber in the Department of Anthropology at Texas State University in San Marcos. We also wish to thank Osmer Balam, Patricia Cukor-Avila, Geneviève Escure, Carol Klee, Mike Linn, Karen López Alonzo, Ron Regal, and Daniela Salcedo for fruitful discussions and insightful comments as we prepared the manuscript for publication.

We thank the University of Minnesota, especially the Global Programs and Strategy Alliance, the Office of the Vice President for Research, and the Institute for Diversity, Equity, and Advocacy for providing financial support for this project. We also thank our respective departments for their ongoing encouragement and enthusiasm for our research, and the University of Minnesota Duluth Geospatial Analysis Institute for preparing the maps of Belize and the Toledo District that appear here. Our gratitude as well to the Institute for Advanced Study at the University of Minnesota for the Residential Faculty Fellowships that provided us with an intellectually charged space in which to write and reflect on our findings. Early analyses of the data were presented at past annual meetings of New Ways of Analyzing Variation, the Linguistic Society of America, the Berkeley Linguistics Society, the Southeastern Conference on

Linguistics, the Chicago Linguistic Society, the Native American and Indigenous Studies Association, and at departmental colloquia at Bucknell University, Carleton University, the University of Minnesota, and the University of North Texas. An earlier version of chapter 2 appeared in the *Journal of Creole and Pidgin Languages* 31.2 (2016), and an earlier version of chapter 4 appeared in *Chicago Linguistic Society* 52 (in press).

Abstract

Is Kriol a minority lg? [handwritten annotation]

Tropical Tongues examines the precarious state of minority languages in coastal Belize, as Kriol has risen to the level of a national language in the period following the country's independence (1981–present). Our fieldwork shows that while the prestige enjoyed by English and Spanish is indisputable, a range of historical and socioeconomic developments have conspired to give Kriol an elevated prestige in the coastal districts at the potential expense of more vulnerable minority languages also spoken there. Our claims are based on ethnographic observations and interviews as well as surveys of language attitudes and use that together show the attenuation of Mopan and Garifuna alongside the stigmatized yet robust Kriol language. Language endangerment studies generally focus on the loss of a minority language to a European language; the present story of language shift and loss examines how large-scale economic restructuring can unsettle existing relationships among minority languages themselves.

KEYWORDS *Latin America; Central America; Belize; Linguistics; Minority Languages; Local Languages; Creole Languages; Mayan Languages; Mopan Language; Garifuna Language; Language Attitudes; Language Ideologies; Language Policy; Language Rights; Language Endangerment*

TROPICAL TONGUES

The Lush Tongues of the Americas

Origin of "prestige": Mid-seventeenth century (in the sense "illusion, conjuring trick"): from French, literally illusion, glamour, from late Latin praestigium *illusion, from Latin* praestigiae *(plural) conjuring tricks. The transference of meaning occurred by way of the sense "dazzling influence, glamour," at first depreciatory.*

—OXFORD ENGLISH DICTIONARY

"Lush": 1. (of vegetation, especially grass) growing luxuriantly: "lush greenery and cultivated fields"; 2. Very rich and providing great sensory pleasure: "lush orchestrations"; 3. Sexually attractive: "She's almost entirely in shadow, but he can see the lush curves of her naked body, the cascading waves of her hair"; 4. Very good or impressive: "I had some really lush pressies [presents]."

—OXFORD ENGLISH DICTIONARY

According to some estimates, almost 6,000 languages are spoken in the roughly 200 countries of the world, with between 550 and 700 languages spoken in the forty-two nations of Latin America and the Caribbean (Campbell 1997, qtd. in AILLA 2017). Spanish, English, Portuguese, French, and Dutch are official languages across this terrain, but they constitute only five of the languages spoken in the region. These European languages have fallen like thin veils over the northernmost, southernmost, easternmost, and westernmost stretches of the Americas, concealing the ubiquity of minority languages throughout the continents. The latter are the lush tongues of the Americas. Exotic at best and at the threshold of extinction at worst, they are the languages spoken in the mountains, the river valleys, the forests, the desert plateaus, the oases, the lowlands, the hills, the grasslands, the marshes and, in the matter that concerns us here, the rimlands of this seemingly endless landscape.[1] One cannot but pause at the thought of how distinct these spaces are from the monolingual national capitals that purportedly represent the diverse ethnolinguistic realities of peoples within the same national borders.

Colonial accounts of the Americas—until the eighteenth-century Bourbon reforms were implemented to promote austerity and so restore the hemorrhaging power of Spain—highlighted the rich variety and abundance of the expansive region. The metaphor of plenitude spilled over into all matters, including the racial, ethnic, and linguistic diversity captured by writers, geographers, botanists, painters, and many other documentarians. These writers' accounts reflected the privileged position of Europeans who marveled at the "products" of the Americas while engaging in bloody and intellectual endeavors to divest the region of those very same "riches." Extensive linguistic diversity was part and parcel of indigenous precontact status, and the process of conquest involved carefully orchestrated projects designed to harness and control the linguistic riches of a "New World" that was already old. Most lush languages were starved, while a small fraction of them were treated with a soft glove at the expense of yet another cluster of lush tongues spoken in the same area.

Relationships between lush languages are less frequently discussed in the language endangerment literature, as the common narrative typically involves endangerment at the hands of a Western European language such as English, Spanish, Portuguese, or French. We know very little about the language ecologies of the lush tongues that defy expectations, and, against all odds, thrive. Before turning to the competing lush tongues of Kriol and Mopan, and Kriol and Garifuna, and the present-day ecologies in which they are situated, it will be useful to consider the larger Latin American history of language contact, change, and shift. In the sections below, we provide brief profiles of lush tongues in coastal Nicaragua, in the larger Mesoamerican context, and in Paraguay, South America's only officially bilingual nation.[2] Each of these linguistic contexts contains its own histories and ecologies, official language policies and grassroots movements. They all nonetheless offer insight into the factors that can lead to the rise of a minority language, the situation we find currently in Belize. The research and literature on these contexts is immense; the descriptions we put forth below, however, are derived from sources that are widely understood as authoritative on the subject matter.

Costeño Languages in Nicaragua

Miskito is one of the oldest languages spoken on the Atlantic Coast of Nicaragua.[3] Like Belize, this coastal strip was a long-standing property of the British, who placed the area under "protection" from 1740 to 1787 as part of the Treaty of Friendship and Alliance with the Miskito Kingdom. Despite their complex relationship to the British and Spanish empires, Miskito peoples retained their cultural and linguistic autonomy for hundreds of years (Helms 1969). The matriarchal organization of families ensured that core groups of Miskito women remained together to raise the children as Miskito in the Miskito language, while their partners—Miskito and British men—traveled and worked elsewhere but sent their earnings to their home base on the coast (Helms 1968). Moravian missionaries appeared in Miskito territory in 1849, translated the Bible to Miskito, and over time became the strongest religious group on the coast, adding a religious layer to concepts of Miskito identity (Dennis 1981). Creole-speaking laborers arrived at about the same time to work on the banana and coconut plantations in Bluefields, Pearl Lagoon, and Little Corn Island.[4] The area remained under British influence until the Miskito Kingdom was formally annexed to the Republic of Nicaragua in 1894. As Charles Hale (1994: 38) explains in his account of the annexation, this was a watershed event that led both the United States and the Nicaraguans to intensify their involvement in the economic and political affairs of the region. It also threw tensions among the six ethnolinguistic coastal communities into sharp relief, particularly those involving Miskito-Creole peoples.[5] Significantly, this event marks the first time that monolingualism was imposed on Bluefields, as armed men entered the town, declaring it the capital of the new Zelaya Department and proclaiming Spanish to be the official language of the Nicaraguan nation (Pineda 2006: 61).

Spanish speakers migrated in large numbers to the Zelaya Department from 1894 forward, though the strip remained largely isolated from the Nicaraguan capital, Managua. When the 1987 Constitution of Nicaragua was signed, it divided the department into two parts—the Región Autónoma de la Costa Caribe Sur and the Región Autónoma de la Costa Caribe Norte—and stated that "the languages of the Communities of the Atlantic Coast shall also be officially used in the cases established by law" even as Spanish would be designated as the official language of the state. The 1987 Constitution, revised in 2004 well after the fall of the Sandinista government, evoked similar sentiments: Chapter VI, Article 89 of the Constitution guaranteed citizens on the Atlantic Coast the same rights, obligations, and protections as its other citizens, as well as autonomy to decide the affairs of the waters and forests of their communal lands.[6] Chapter VI, Articles 90 and 91 addressed minority languages directly:

> Article 90: The communities of the Atlantic Coast have the right to free expression and preservation of their languages, art, and culture. The development of their culture and their values enriches the national culture. The state shall create special programs to enhance the exercise of these rights.

> Article 91: The state has the obligation to enact laws intended to promote actions to ensure that no Nicaraguan shall be the object of discrimination for reasons of language, culture, or origin.

Under the Sandinista government, linguists and language activists worked in tandem with the communities on the Atlantic Coast to document and preserve the languages spoken in the area. Article 121 of the Constitution stated that "communities of the Atlantic Coast have access in the region to education in their maternal languages to levels that are determined in accordance with national plans and programs." Thus, despite having been incorporated into the broader revolutionary nation, there was a grassroots language rights movement that actively encouraged the use and appreciation of minority languages of the revolutionary nation.

Under the succeeding administration led by President Violeta Chamorro, a five-year bilingual intercultural education plan (1992–96) was put in place on the Atlantic Coast (Arnove and Ovando 1993: 147–51). Government policy and grassroots movements for autonomy have led to discussions about language rights that continue to take place on the Atlantic Coast to this day (Freeland 2011). Yet throughout these discussions, the vitality of Nicaragua Creole English eventually superseded the vitality of Miskito, to the point that the latter is seeing an increasing loss of speakers as transmission to younger generations diminishes and children turn to Creole as a symbol of Atlantic Coast identity, viewing it as a means to emerge from the long-standing poverty and isolation that has characterized the coast throughout much of its history.

The Minority Languages of Mesoamerica

The area that was once British Honduras and is known today as Belize was once part of a larger area known as Mesoamerica. Since the term *Mesoamerica* was first used to describe the region that today comprises central and southern Mexico and northern Central America, it has been defined in geographic and linguistic terms that capture the cultural connections of the peoples who inhabited the region before the arrival of the Spanish. The linguistic diversity of the area cannot be dismissed.[7] As Shirley Heath (1972) writes, over eighty languages and dialects were spoken in the Valley of Mexico alone upon Hernán Cortés's arrival in Tenochtitlán—the land of abundant prickly pears over rock. Nahuatl, however, had a prominent position over the other lush tongues in the area since it was used in commerce, trade, and the Aztec judicial system. In such a rich site of cultural and linguistic exchange, Mayan peoples had already been "Mexicanized and Toltecized before they were ever Hispanicized" (Lutz 1976: 50). The Nahuatl language's reach in the Guatemalan Highlands had been so extensive that neither the *Anales de los Cakchiqueles/Annals of the Caqchiquels* (Hernández

Arana Xajilá 1953 [1507]) nor Pedro de Alvarado's letters to Hernán Cortés (1524) suggest that Spaniards faced any difficulty communicating with the leaders of the five Mayan kingdoms during their invasion of the territory (de Alvarado 1924). Yet as R. McKenna Brown (1998: 58) notes, ultimately, Spanish language policy would vary greatly in New Spain and the Kingdom of Guatemala: in the former, Nahuatl became the vernacular and lingua franca, and in the latter, Spaniards manipulated the ethnic and language differences among the five highland Mayan communities in order to better divide and conquer the area.

Despite the official monolingual policy of Spanish King Charles V between 1521 and 1565, the Nahuatl linguistic community in New Spain grew in the sixteenth and seventeenth centuries and came to include not only ethnic Nahuatl speakers, but also Dominican and Franciscan friars, Peninsulares, Criollos, and Mestizos who spoke it with varying degrees of linguistic fluency and competence (Parodi 2006: 39). Its growth was organic—due to marriages across castes in the valley, insurrections in areas like the Yucatán that the Spanish attempted and failed to conquer, and the widespread isolation of areas of little interest to Spaniards in their quest for gold and resources—and it became clear that monolingualism could not thrive. Spanish King Phillip II's declaration in 1570 that Nahuatl would be the official language of the "Indians" in New Spain marked a novel approach to linguistic policy: in the Kingdom of Guatemala, at least eight edicts reminding and reprimanding friars for not using Mayan languages were sent as policy reminders between 1575 and 1629 (McKenna Brown 1998: 57). Spanish King Phillip IV revoked the indigenous language policy just six years before his death in 1634.

Thenceforth, there began a remarkable exchange between the Crown, which took up again the claim that Castilian would be the language of New Spain, and friars, who responded to their edicts with detailed accounts of the emerging diglossic linguistic reality—Nahuatl-speaking families across castes, the growing use of Nahuatl between women and the extensive use of Castilian in public and government spheres (Parodi 2006: 47). Nahuatl was *the* vernacular and lingua franca of New Spain:[8] by the end of the colonial period, only 35 percent of the population of New Spain spoke Castilian and only 0.5 percent could write and read in it (Hidalgo 2001: 59). In the Captaincy General of Guatemala, Kaqchikel[9] could have attained a similar position since the friars who were charged with administering the newly created towns continued to use indigenous languages, particularly Kaqchikel, as the language of administration and linguistic/religious instruction (Van Oss 1986: 18). There were crucial differences in the historical contexts, though. Nahuatl was, in effect, a symbol of a prized colonial identity that made New Spain "special" among the other Spanish colonies, much like we would see in casta paintings of the pre-Bourbon period. It highlighted the many ways that Mexico was golden, supple, plentiful, and abundant, in sharp contrast to decaying, corrupt, and old Spain. However, unlike Nahuatl in New Spain, the repercussions of speaking Kaqchikel or any other Mayan language became severe after Phillip IV's declaration. In 1646, Royal Visitor Antonio de Lara ordered indigenous people to assume Spanish patronymic names, learn Spanish, and presented only "Indians" who learned Spanish with the "privilege" of wearing European clothing and riding bridled horses (Aguirre 1972: 373–74, qtd. in Becker Richards and Richards 1997). Although there were a great number of Kaqchikel speakers in the Captaincy of Guatemala, the linguistic community remained entrenched in the lowest socioeconomic sector and was severely punished for not shifting to monolingual Castilian.

While the colonial project led to the decimation of indigenous communities in New Spain and the Captaincy General of Guatemala, it was the linguistic policy imposed on the eve of independence that dealt the crushing blow to the lush tongues spoken in what became Mexico and Central America. Influenced by the positivism of the period, leaders in the new Republic of Guatemala called for an eradication of Mayan languages in 1824 (Becker Richards and Richards 1997: 195). Meanwhile, a similar postindependence spirit was altering the place of Nahuatl in Mexico. Formed in 1875, the Mexican branch of the Real Academia de Española officially proclaimed the Mexican variety of Spanish to be the official language of the nation: "no la [lengua] española pura, sino la española modelada por nuestro medio físico y social" (Castillo 1965: 109). Linguistic policy became evermore strict in the aftermath of the Mexican Revolution, as leaders openly sought to extinguish indigenous languages (Cabrera 1935: 19; Klee and Lynch 2009: 119). In the 1940s, Guatemala and Mexico both created National Indigenist Institutes in order to address the "Indian Problem" (Becker Richards and Richards 1997). Since then, "bilingual" educational policies have followed a cycle of development, implementation, and revision, all with the objective to "Castilianize the Indian" in Mexico and Guatemala (Becker Richards and Richards 1997; McKenna Brown 1998). Despite linguistic discrimination, however, the number of self-identified bilinguals in Mexico and Guatemala has risen since the 1940s (Klee and Lynch 2009; Cifuentes and Moctezuma 2006).[10]

In both countries, two critical sociohistorical developments affected the position of indigenous languages. In Mexico, the 1994 Zapatista insurrection highlighted the historical marginalization of the country's southern indigenous populations, while at the same time reigniting conversations about indigenous autonomy (Hidalgo 2006; Vásquez Carranza 2009).[11] The San Andrés Larráinzar Accords led to constitutional reforms detailing the rights of indigenous communities in Mexico, which then led to the Ley General de Derechos Lingüísticos de los Pueblos Indígenas (General Law on Linguistic Rights of Indigenous People, 2003; see Cámera de Diputados 2015), which declared in Article 3 that indigenous languages were cultural and linguistic national patrimony. This document went on to specify how these languages would be recognized, protected, and promoted in both public and private spheres. Similar legislation was adopted in Guatemala on the heels of the 1996 peace accords, when the government adopted as official policy language regarding multilingualism and Mayan identity (Fishman and García 2010). The Ley Nacional de Idiomas Nacionales (Law of National Languages, 2003), reinforced Spanish as the official language of Guatemala before stating the actions the Guatemalan government would take—in some cases in tandem with the Academia de Lenguas Mayas de Guatemala—to recognize, promote, and respect the languages of Mayan, Garifuna, and Xinca communities (Congreso de la República de Guatemala 2003).

While some of the minority languages in Mexico and Guatemala enjoy "vigorous" language use, with continued transmission across generations, negative attitudes toward these languages can be quite prevalent across the middle and upper classes of these countries. There remains a glass ceiling for speakers of indigenous languages, rendering it virtually impossible for them to ascend into positions of power in the public sphere. This is in spite of the fact that many speakers of indigenous languages now possess levels of education comparable to that of the middle and upper strata. Despite the policies adopted in 2003 in Guatemala and Mexico, the vitality of indigenous communities across Mesoamerica continues to depend on a high concentration of speakers across age groups residing in isolated areas, far from predominantly monolingual Spanish-speaking, Mestizo/Ladino-governed cultural centers.

Four Pillars in Paraguay

The question of a glass ceiling for speakers of lush tongues—ever present in the contexts we have examined, and duplicated in areas like the Andes where grassroots activism is vigorous and yet multiculturalist legislation has been passed—brings the conversation full circle to the matter of linguistic ideologies.[12] Neither grassroots social movements nor multiculturalist legislation alone are enough to ensure that a lush tongue will be transmitted from one generation to another, or that the community of speakers will expand to assure its vitality. Like an object that cannot stand alone from the sum of its parts, the viability of lush tongues fundamentally depends on several factors. These include (1) the prestige of the language across social classes and across generations, (2) an organic impetus to protect and preserve the language emerging from the community itself, (3) an abstract idea about the language as a core aspect of individual and national identity, and (4) a national investment in seeing that the language thrives. In the Americas, there is but one location where the four pillars supporting a lush tongue have resulted in its vitality and incorporation into the national fabric: Paraguay.

Guaraní was one of several languages spoken in what is now Paraguay before the arrival of Portuguese colonists (*Ethnologue* 2017b). The area was not of interest to the Spanish Crown, given the absence of precious metals and the difficulty of establishing communication between it and the Viceroyalty of Peru (Klee and Lynch 2009: 10).[13] These factors contributed to the region's unique sociocultural development, which then established a unique sociolinguistic context. In this space, there were very few European women, thus European men often married native women who spoke Guaraní to their children and taught it to their husbands (Rubin 1974). Trade and religion were carried out in Guaraní, and, given Jesuit interest in the language during their stay in the colony (1604–1767), the standardization of Guaraní and the development of a literary tradition occurred under the auspices of the priests. Paraguay experienced almost complete isolation from the colonial period through the mid-nineteenth century (Choi 2000). Guaraní then became a symbol of "national unity" during two important wars—the Guerra Grande (1865–70) and the Guerra del Chaco (1932–35)—though the wars themselves put an end to the long-lived isolation of the area and ushered in the growing influence of Spanish as Paraguay underwent demographic changes as a result of fatalities, migration, and the forced displacement of its peoples. Guaraní was long held as a symbol of national identity, and bilingual Paraguayans often used it in familiar, intimate contexts while reserving Spanish for formal situations, including the educational and political spheres (Rubin 1974).

The conversation about the place of Guaraní in the public and private spheres of Paraguayan life is at least four decades old now. As Shaw Gynan (2007) explains, Guaraní was first proposed as an official language at the 1967 National Constitutional Convention. While the measure was unanimously rejected, the discussion about the participants' appreciation for the language led to the designation of both Spanish and Guaraní as national languages, with the former designated as the official language, in Article 5 of the Constitution. Six years later, in May 1972, President Alfredo Stroessner issued Decree 26,420, highlighting the status of Guaraní in the discourse of bilingualism that was gaining steam in the country: "Guaraní constitutes the most highly valued cultural patrimony of our country and it is the duty of every Paraguayan to learn it, disseminate it, and enrich it since it is the vernacular Language of our land"

(Gynan 2007: 265). When the discussion about the place of Guaraní arose at the 1992 Constitutional Convention, it was accepted as an official language without debate and language was readily incorporated into the Constitution to mark Paraguay's status as a "pluricultural" and "bilingual" country. In contrast to other contexts in the region, Tadeo Zarratea notes, "the construction of a bilingual Paraguay means bilingualising the State, the educational system, and the press. It is not about bilingualising the people, who, as we have stated previously, have their bilingualism and even their diglossia as undeniable truths" (Zarratea 1995, qtd. in Gynan 2007: 266). Thus, institutional language attitudes were already strongly in favor of a prominent position for Guaraní as politicians, educators, and journalists undertook the task of formally recognizing the de facto place of Guaraní in their spheres.

Guaraní is one of several lush tongues spoken in Paraguay, but it is also the language that Korean immigrants use with their customers in Asunción, and it is the language spoken by foreign diplomats at cocktail parties. As brazen as it might seem to say, its importance is confirmed in the words of those same immigrants who state, "We'd go broke if we didn't know the basics," and in former U.S. ambassador James Cason's astute move to become fluent in the language and record a Guaraní folk song that landed him a spot on the airwaves (Romero 2012). Despite the presence of the many lush tongues spoken for millennia in Paraguay's Chaco region, and despite the fact that the last census recorded a small percentage of ethnic Guaraní people, it is the only language besides Spanish that has been nourished by a steady production of literature—from poetry during the colonial Jesuit missions, to the diglossia captured in Augusto Roas Bastos's *Yo, El Supremo* during the Latin American Boom literary movement, to contemporary translations of *Don Quixote* and the *Book of Mormon*. As Articles 77 and 140 of the 2010 Constitution state:

Article 77, Of Teaching in the Mother Tongue: Teaching at the beginning of the educational process will be performed in the official mother tongue of the student. They will also be instructed in the knowledge and the use of both official languages of the

Republic. In the case of ethnic minorities whose language is not Guaraní, it will be possible to choose either of the two official languages.

Article 140, Of the Languages: Paraguay is a multicultural and bilingual country. Castilian and Guaraní are official languages. The law will establish the modalities for using one and the other. The indigenous languages, as well as those of other minorities, are part of the cultural patrimony of the Nation.

While other lush tongues spoken in the country are recognized as cultural patrimony, the rise of Guaraní to official language status has solidified its place as the eminent marker of national identity, at the expense of other indigenous languages spoken in the country. And it is at school that a younger generation faces the constitutional mandate to select between Guaraní and Spanish as the only two possibilities for language of instruction.

Belize isn't Latin America

The Tropical Tongues of Belize

Though it is beyond the scope of this book to examine the language attitudes across the Americas from the colonial period to the present in a manner that does them justice, the preceding sections have offered a glimpse of the fluctuating prestige of lush tongues across multiple contexts in Latin America. In these cases, political and socioeconomic factors have transpired at different moments in the region's history to nourish lush tongues, often at the expense of others in their midst. Despite the variety of situations and contexts, one underlying theme is that language policy (and its effective implementation), grassroots language movements, ideologies about the linguistic core of individual and group identity, and language attitudes have *together* had an impact and ensure the consistent and ongoing linguistic vitality of lush tongues, from the colonial period to the present day. The history of language attitude research in Latin America and the Caribbean itself is limited, and we endeavor to highlight aspects of the question that remain obscure. Previous research on language endangerment, language policy, language rights movements, and language attitudes has been concerned with relations between the minority/majority or creole/vernacular languages and the linguistic standard of individual countries or regions. Our interdisciplinary inquiry into the relationship between the lush languages of the Belizean coast deepens the conversation by shedding light on socioeconomic factors that pressure language change. Factors like the transition from an agricultural/fishing economy to a service economy, which would be considered peripheral in many studies of language change, are central in our narrative. In this analysis, macro- and microeconomic factors are paramount in accelerating the rise of prestige of one lush tongue over others spoken in the same geographic area.

The dynamic nature of language—its constant change and evolution—has long been a topic of interest in linguistics and anthropology, and research in this area has produced important results: from directly challenging prescriptive ideas about "correct" and "incorrect" speech, to providing insight into relationships between languages, to closer examination of the kinds of internal and external pressures that are often at work in language shift and change.[14] There has been significant research investigating internal motivations of language change, which occurs as a result of structural properties of the language itself: for example, the regularization of irregular forms.[15] Similarly, external motivations for language change, which occur as a result of contact between differing linguistic communities, have also been well documented, with creole languages being the example par excellence.[16] So, it is clear that external motivations—that is, contact with another language—can play an important role in structural innovations within a given language.

For some researchers, however, such as Salikoko Mufwene (2007, inter alia), all language change is motivated by external forces: "All language changes are externally-motivated, in the sense that the motivation for, or causation of, change is external to language structure, and contact (situated at the idiolectal level) has always been an important factor causing changes in the 'balance of power' among competing variants" (66). The language change we are concerned with in our research—specifically language shift and endangerment—is unquestionably a result of external motivations and language contact. Contact has been the rule in coastal Belize for centuries. The particular stories we tell here, however, have their origins in the nineteenth century. The stories involve migration and slavery and the languages of the Mopan Maya,[17] the Garifuna, the Creoles, and the English colonizers. They are also a product of the twenty-first century, as a confluence of economic and political factors have conspired over the last several decades to elevate Kriol, with the perhaps unintended result of pushing the Mopan and Garifuna languages rapidly toward endangerment.

Chapter One

The Languages of Belize in Context

Belize—formerly British Honduras—gained full independence from Great Britain in 1981. While there is a strong influence of English as a result of its colonial history and the large levels of immigration to and from the United States, Belize is linguistically diverse. According to the 2010 Belizean census, there are at least ten languages spoken in Belize, including Chinese, English, Garifuna, German, Kriol, Maya Kekchi, Maya Mopan, Maya Yucatec, and Spanish. This is significant in a country the size of Belize, which has a population of only 300,000. It is only in the last thirty years, though, that Kriol has become something like the national language. As researchers have noted, Kriol is and has been important as a marker of Belizean identity, and in the face of these pressures it has developed even further as a sign of one's true Belizeanness (Le Page 1992; Ravindranath 2009). Belize is very much a country in flux, and Kriol seems more than ever to be a marker of traditional Belizean identity (Salmon and Gómez Menjívar 2014, 2016).

There are relatively few studies on the linguistic situation of Belize. The most extensive fieldwork on Kriol was conducted by Geneviève Escure (1981, 1991, 1997) in Placencia in the late 1970s and early 1980s, long before the coastal town became a booming tourist hub that today draws Hondurans, Salvadorans, Creoles, and Garifuna to its many foreign-owned businesses and hotels, including one by the famous movie director Francis Ford Coppola. More recently, Maya Ravindranath (2009) has examined language change and language shift in Hopkins, a Garifuna community. Bruce Ergood (1996), Timothy Hagerty (1996), and Osmer Balam (2015) have examined Belizean Spanish and code-switching in the Corozal, Cayo, and Orange Walk Districts of Belize.[1] The present study contributes to existing research by examining the current status of the minority languages spoken in coastal Belize, grounding our research in systematic field research in order to provide a fresh account of language endangerment in this dynamic area.

Prior to independence, many ethnolinguistic communities in Belize could be understood as "language islands."[2] As Hildo do Couto (2014: 176) explains in his study of Amerindian language islands in Brazil, this term "suggests that the *territory of the relevant population (with its language)* is a kind of island within another population (with its culture and language) analogized as an ocean. Further, it implies that there is a hinterland from which the 'island' is somehow detached and to which it remains related" (emphasis ours). Like do Couto, we believe that this image, better than the term *enclave* employed most often in Anglophone and Romance linguistics, illustrates the status and condition of minority language communities before waves of socioeconomic change begin to erode their shores.[3] Over the last three decades, the Belizean economy has swiftly transitioned from a traditional maritime and agricultural economy to a global, service-based economy that ebbs and flows with the arrival of flights and cruise ships to its seaside towns. This provides advantageous economic opportunities for women and minorities in the districts closest to tourist hot spots. Along with the economic opportunities, however, there is a real impact on the minority languages spoken in the country, as young speakers turn toward the language(s) they perceive as economically favorable, which in this case is Kriol and, to a lesser extent, Belizean English.

Fieldwork on the Belizean Coast

When we first arrived in Belize in 2012, our intention was to study the conventions of language and language practice among speakers of Belizean Kriol, an English-based creole spoken in coastal Belize. Our goal was to investigate linguistic variation in Kriol between speakers from coastal villages and cays and those in the country's urban center, Belize City, where the majority of ethnic Kriol speakers reside. The project was tied into a rapidly growing area of inquiry in linguistics that extends current thought in pragmatics and semantics to questions of discourse, presupposition, and politeness in indigenous and non-English languages. Kriol, with its Amerindian and African influences, offered a perfect vehicle for continuing this kind of work. William Salmon (2014, 2016) used directly elicited data, interviews with native speakers of Kriol, and the *Kriol-Inglish Dikshineri* (Herrera et al. 2010), published as a collaborative effort between the Belize Kriol Project and the Belize Ministry of Education, to respond to these linguistic questions.

Our fieldwork took an interdisciplinary turn when we deliberated on the extensive use and spread of Kriol throughout coastal Belize across ethnic groups. Traveling southward down the coast gave us insight into a hitherto undocumented linguistic context undergoing great socioeconomic and demographic changes. Escure (1991) predicted that the influx of Spanish-speaking immigrants from neighboring Central American countries would cause Belizeans to stop using Kriol as the lingua franca in their country. This belief was widespread, and even appeared as the front-page headline of Belize's largest-circulation newspaper, *Amandala*, on September 11, 1992: "Belize Now *Belice*." Two months later, the *New York Times* ran an article titled "Without Firing a Shot, Espanol [*sic*] Captures Belize." Yet Kriol was very much alive in Belize City, Placencia, the Cayes, and Punta Gorda. It was the language used by newly arrived Spanish-speaking immigrants, Chinese shopkeepers, Mayan college students, U.S.-born teen missionaries speaking with locals, and Mennonites haggling with Mayan women in the market. Kriol was not only alive; its heart was racing.

As we began to take the pulse of Kriol, it became necessary to examine how its rhythm altered the pace of language change in other languages with which it was in contact. As a result, the study required moving beyond standard distinctions between majority and minority languages (also known as local languages) and extending beyond standard conventions in the study of language attitudes.[4] Our fieldwork dialogues with the existing research in linguistics and Latin American studies on language contact, language endangerment, language ideologies, and grassroots language rights movements. It nonetheless represents a significant departure in the theorization of these matters through its focus on socioeconomic factors contributing to language change and overall language ecology (Mufwene 2001, 2003). After all, while pride and prestige are certainly factors contributing to Kriol's vitality, they are not the only driving forces of language change across that lush coastal strip.

Methodology

Belize is divided into six districts: Corozal, Orange Walk, Cayo, Belize, Stann Creek, and Toledo (map 1). We conducted fieldwork in the major cultural centers of these latter three districts, specifically in Belize City (the former colonial capital and current Creole cultural capital), Seine Bight (one of the oldest Garifuna villages), Placencia and Ambergris Cay (the fastest-growing tourist destinations in the country and the sites with the most pull factors attracting immigrants from neighboring Central American countries), Belmopan (Belize's national capital and the home of a sizeable Mestizo population), Punta Gorda (one of the two access points to neighboring Guatemala), and San Antonio Village (the first homeland in Belize for the Mopan Mayan community). In selecting these sites, we aimed to cover the linguistic context of the northern, southern, and central reaches of coastal Belize, the area with the least contact with Spanish.[5]

We followed methods that were best suited to the sociocultural conditions of the ethnic minority communities in question, relying upon experimental and ethnographic methods as well as direct surveys as was fitting in the various contexts. We are quite aware of the problems a researcher's presence in a social situation can raise with respect to the quality of the data, and we were careful to minimize these effects as much as possible.[6] We proceeded as well with the understanding of Mopan and Garifuna communities as former language islands, which are formidable sites from which to observe the effects of language contact, including the factors that lead to moribundity and language extinction (do Couto 2014: 76–77). Language islands possess unique characteristics, for they are "comunidades lingüísticas em espaços delimitados, com línguas ou varie-

Map 1. Belize.
Courtesy of the UMD
Geospatial Analysis
Center, Map data
BERDS, Esri.

dades que se distinguem de modo relativamente claro da língua do entorno, e nas quais há uma consciência da própria alteridade, baseada em uma densa rede de comunicação . . . , e que se dirige mais para dentro do que para fora" (Rosenberg 2003, ctd. in do Couto 2007: 318).[7] During the course of our fieldwork we came to understand that the parameters of these linguistic islands were experiencing erosion and that macroeconomic factors are changing the formerly inwardly focused orientation of the Mopan and Garifuna communities; it became paramount for us to work with community members during data collection.

Given the widespread use of Kriol English in Belize City, we did not expect to encounter any complications in soliciting opinions about Kriol from residents there. Many Belize City residents are accustomed to meeting tourists and sharing cultural information about Belize, its language, its most impressive sights and differences between the country and the United States, and so on. In this context, it was clear that experimental methods such as the verbal guise test would not be intrusive or inappropriate. Accordingly, we designed a four-speaker verbal guise test and questionnaire to examine attitudes toward two varieties of Kriol.[8] Our participants listened to two pairs of recordings—in the first pair, speakers told an Anansi story and in the second pair, speakers related a personal story. These recordings were approximately thirty seconds each and were provided by native Kriol speakers who were alike in sex, age, occupation, and in being lifelong residents of their respective hometowns. Each was recorded in natural conversation with the male researcher. The questionnaires consisted of a five-level modified Likert survey, which queried sixteen personality traits. We surveyed a total of 141 participants. At the end of the interview, participants completed qualitative questions about Kriol as well as questions on the participants' own linguistic backgrounds. The interviews took five to thirty minutes per participant.

With respect to the Mopan language, we had determined based on earlier trips to Toledo District that the community we wished to survey would require a very different set of instruments than those used in the Kriol contexts of Belize City and Punta Gorda. Mayan communities are located in less frequented areas where foreign visitors tend to be missionaries,[9] or academics conducting research on language, environment, or farming.[10] Language issues are important to this group, but many Mayas are reluctant to share their views with outsiders. As such, we believed the experimental methods described above with the verbal guise test would be less effective—and possibly distracting—in this context. We instead constructed direct surveys to gather the attitudinal data we needed. With the assistance of a fluent speaker of Mopan recommended by elders in the community, we queried thirty-eight participants about Mopan and English, with another forty participants responding to questions about Mopan and Kriol. The surveys consisted of two parts: the first covered demographic information, such as sex, age, ethnic identification, parents' occupations, and the participant's degree of fluency in any languages they indicated they knew. Participants then responded to language-attitude and language-use questions on a five-level modified Likert scale. The questions specifically asked participants to consider the use of Mopan in educational settings, language and ethnic identity, language and context, and language and the participant's future.

The final phase of our research focused on the Garifuna language of Seine Bight village in Stann Creek District. We had arranged to stay with a Garifuna family while in Seine Bight, but the family notified us upon our arrival in town that they could not host us because the room was still under construction. Nonetheless, they invited us to visit their home and warmly introduced us to their friends and family around the village. It soon became apparent that the Garifuna language was not frequently used in the village, and with the help of the family and friends we revised our surveys in wording and target content. In addition, inspired by anthropologist Richard Wilk's (1999) work in Belize City, we included a door-to-door approach to our survey distribution method. We collected approximately fifty in-depth surveys in this manner, though the "door-to-door" nature of the process was frequently quite different from what the term suggests. Often, for example, one participant would introduce us to another, or take us to visit another house across the village where we could talk to more residents. In another situation, we were invited to hang out with a participant in his workshop while he constructed maracas out of calabash gourd and weinwein seeds. This particular participant never did fill out the survey, but he talked for the better part of the morning about the language and village history. Chapter 4 is thus based on a pairing of quantitative survey data and qualitative observations made throughout Seine Bight and neighboring Placencia.

Belizean Minority Languages in Contact

Language contact can have implications for the structure of the languages in question: that is, innovations in a recipient language can be influenced by features of a source language. Another common result of language contact, however, is bi- or multilingualism. In this case, the communities in contact have political, cultural, economic, or other reasons for maintaining their native language at the same time as learning the language of their neighbors in contact. In some situations, what can result is a state frequently referred to as "stable bilingualism." In such instances, bilingual speakers might use one language for certain topics and the other language for other topics.[11] For example, Utta von Gleich and Wolfgang Wölck (1994, 2001) and Wölck (2008) describe the Quechua-Spanish relation in Bolivia, Ecuador, and Peru, in which Quechua is used for some topics and Spanish for others. As long as this state of linguistic "compartmentalism" persists, both languages can continue to survive, as there are domains of need and use for both. However, as Joshua Fishman (1970: 78, qtd. in Wölck 2008) warns, "were the roles not compartmentalized, i.e., were they not kept separate by dint of association with quite separate (though complementary) values, domains of activity, and everyday situations, one language (or variety) would displace the other as role and value distinctions merged and became blurred." The situation Fishman describes is more likely to occur in instances where the social status (along various dimensions) of one language group declines in relation to the other. What follows is a reduction in the number of domains of use in which that language is accepted. As Wölck (2008) writes, "Unless the social status of the minority population improves, the (few) domains appropriate to their language will . . . gradually and successfully be invaded by the majority language." This state is often referred to as "transitional bilingualism," in which a community gradually moves from speaking two languages to using only the language of the majority or dominant population, a process that can result in near or complete language loss in as soon as two or three generations.[12] This transitional situation is what we see in Belize with the Mopan and Garifuna languages.

European languages enjoy relatively parallel prestige in Latin America for obvious geopolitical reasons. Conversely, the lush tongues of the Americas suffer a status more akin to stigmatization and very few cases exist where macro- and microeconomic forces have converged to promote their ascendance in linguistic hierarchies. This is one. Our research, based on fieldwork conducted from 2012 to 2016, indicates that as the Kriol language gains acceptance and is spoken in an ever-larger number of situations and contexts, Mopan and Garifuna linguistic islands contract in terms of size of territory and number of speakers whose socioeconomic futures can sustain the linguistic compartmentalism previous generations were able to maintain.

Chapter Two

Kriol

From Minority to National Language

Ideas about what constituted a "creole" heritage in Belize were fluid from the mid-seventeenth century until the first decades of the twentieth century, when a sort of consensus was reached as to what the term would mean in Belize: "There were a variety of different ent groups that collectively were consolidated as 'Belizean Creole' between 1650 and 1930: slaves brought to British Honduras from Africa (either directly, or, much more commonly, through Jamaica); 'Creole' slaves (slaves born in the Caribbean); free black, free colored and European settlers, these latter three groups of freed people each encompassing an array of socio-economic statuses, from wealthy slave owners to poor renegades" (Johnson 2003: 602). Despite the array of origins, historical trajectories, and material circumstances, ethnic Creoles spoke a vernacular language that bound them together: Kriol. While the debates about the origins of creole languages in the Americas are extensive, scholars in general concur that creole languages originated through slavery-induced language contact, whether in the Caribbean or West Africa. Belizean Kriol is no different, and it was likely carried to Belize from Jamaica by slaves who were brought to work in Belizean logging camps. Much of the slave population in seventeenth-, eighteenth-, and nineteenth-century Belize came through Jamaica, and Belizean and Jamaican Creole overlap significantly today.[1] Not surprisingly, Ken Decker (2005: 3) proposes that prior to 1787, Belizean Kriol was in fact even closer to Jamaican Creole than it is today. Belizean Kriol is thus an English-based creole, and scholars have identified West African substrate languages such as Akan, Efik, Ewe, Fula, Ga, Hausa, Igbo, Kikongo, and Wolof in its structure and lexicon.

While the accounts from local communities are often not considered in scholarly literature, we wish to note that for the Belizeans of all backgrounds we met throughout the course of this research, this is *the* origin story of Kriol.

The year 1838 marked the end of slavery in Belize and throughout the British Empire. Until then, Garifuna and Mayan communities had remained outside of the colonial economic web of relationships, since they resided in sites of intensified British presence—logging areas and ports in the northern part of the country. That came to an end in 1872, when colonists imposed the Crown Lands Ordinance, which established reservations for Mayan and Garifuna communities and prevented these groups from owning land. After this point, the Creole ethnic group in British Honduras held an intermediary position between Europeans and other minorities as the former masters expanded the logging industry into the interior and south of the country. These socioeconomic relationships remained relatively unchallenged throughout the *longue durée* of British Honduras's colonial period (1872–1981), and Kriol began to be used as a lingua franca very early, especially in logging areas.

The place of Kriol in colonial British Honduras has largely determined its place after Belize's independence: it benefits from a historically favorable position that has only been accentuated after 1981, though at the same time, it continues to be regarded as simply "broken English" born in the context of slavery and colonialism. Yet, as Robert Le Page (1992 [1998: 75]) observed nearly four decades ago, "The Creoles of Belize said similar derogatory things about their language within the context of education [but] nevertheless called it Creole and identified themselves, with pride and feelings of superiority, as Creoles."[2] In this chapter we discuss covert and overt language attitudes toward two varieties of Kriol spoken in Belize, the vitality of the language and its maintenance as the irrefutable national language of Belize, particularly in the wake of mass Creole emigration out of Belize.

Kriol is the native language of many Belizeans, regardless of their ethnic group. For example, Escure (1997) notes that Kriol "competes with Spanish as an indicator of youth solidarity and interethnic solidarity among Yucatec Maya and Mestizo youth in the Corazal district." More recently, Balam (2013) demonstrates that code-switching between Kriol, Spanish, and English is very common in Orange Walk District because speakers associate it with their multi-lingual identities. Yet, Balam notes that younger secondary school speakers are beginning to employ more Kriol, at the expense of Northern Belizean Spanish and even code-switching. The trend "may be pointing to the genesis of a strong pan-Afro-Belizean linguistic identity among younger Belizeans which cuts across ethnic lines, and which consequently holds implications for issues of language dominance, language shift, and language policy and planning in Belize" (Balam 2013: 247).

In our own research on the place of Kriol in coastal areas, we have observed the extensive reach of Kriol—it is the language used in stores owned by Chinese Belizeans throughout the coast; it is the language adopted by the Guatemalan, Honduran, and Salvadoran immigrants who work on the streets of Belize City, the Cayes and Placencia Beach; it is the first language of our youngest Mayan participants in Toledo District; and it is frequently the first or second language of Garifuna peoples in Seine Bight, Dangriga, Hopkins, and Punta Gorda. It is, nonetheless, commonly derided by many of its speakers—regardless of their ethnic background—as merely "broken English." This might be due to speakers' intuitions that much of the vocabulary—approximately 88 percent, according to John Holm (1977)—is shared with Standard English.[3] At the same time, however, the phonology and syntax of Kriol mark it off as distinctly not Standard English, which leads to the impression of it as a deficient variety of the majority, lexifying English.[4]

Our informal conversations with numerous Belizeans in Belize City, Caye Caulker, Belmopan, Placencia, and Punta Gorda revealed the rich complexity of attitudes toward Kriol. There is pride in the language and in independent Belize, yet this was consistently undermined by warnings that Kriol was not good English. We first encountered this seeming incongruence of attitudes in Belize City, the Creole cultural capital of Belize, and we wondered if it would be the same elsewhere in the country. To answer this question, we designed a verbal guise study to tease apart these attitudes in Belize City, as well as in Punta Gorda, which is the largest town in the country's south.[5] In Belize City, we surveyed in downtown Belize City (Albert Street, King Street, Regent Street, etc.), the Vernon Street fish market, Michael Finnegan Market, Fort George, Queen Street, Freetown, all along Barrack Road, and on the campus of the University of Belize in Belize City. In Punta Gorda, we surveyed people around the central park, on Main Street, the Front Street market, the Punta Gorda hospital, the airstrip, Maya Island Air and Tropic Air ticket counters, the University of Belize campus in Punta Gorda, as well as in various homes and businesses in the city. We surveyed Belizeans of many ethnicities, including ethnic Creoles, East Indians, Garifunas, Mestizos, Kekchi and Mopan Mayas, and Central American immigrants. Essentially, we surveyed members of almost every major group except Mennonites. As a result, we spoke with Belizeans from a wide variety of professional and ethnic backgrounds—from lawyers to insurance salespeople to security guards and police officers, to street vendors, store clerks, fisherman, taxi drivers, and university students. Indeed, our pool was as diverse and complex as the population of Belize itself.

Our aim here was to go beyond the "standard" view in the literature of the relations between creoles and their lexifying languages and instead try to understand the factors that have contributed to Kriol's prestige, and how its appeal might vary across ethnic groups, and between men and women.[6] We surveyed a total of 141 participants with equal numbers of men and women, and our participant pool closely resembled the ethnic group distribution in each locale: in Belize City (71 total participants), 91.45 percent of our participants identified as native speakers of Kriol, 7.04 percent were native speakers of Spanish, and 1.40 percent were native speakers of Garifuna; in Punta Gorda (70 participants), 57.74 percent were native speakers of Kriol, 4.28 percent were native speakers of Spanish, 17.14 percent were native speakers of Mopan, 15.71 percent were speakers of Kekchi, and 4.28 percent were native speakers of Garifuna. Our pool also ranged across socioeconomic classes, including college students, professionals and semiprofessionals working in doctors' offices and medical clinics, lawyers' offices, government offices, as well as taxi drivers, restaurant and hotel staff, fishermen, street vendors, security guards, and retail clerks.

To run the verbal guise test, we recorded two ethnic Creole men telling Anansi stories and two other ethnic Creole men telling stories about their youth—one chose to tell a story about his grandfather and the other told a story about fishing.[7] Our goal in this diversity of recordings was twofold. First, we wanted the speech to which test participants were exposed to be more natural than, say, a recording of someone reading prepared written passages aloud, as is commonly done in verbal guise tests. Second, with the inclusion of the Anansi stories, we wanted to gather attitudes across two different genres of speech—one of which was personal and conversational and one of which was the Belizean folk tale.

We then asked these participants to rate the speakers on a series of traits as they listened to the stories, and to tell us where they thought the men they heard in the recording resided. Kriol was well regarded by participants in both locations, though all of the participants found the Belize City variety of Kriol more appealing than the Punta Gorda variety. This was true of traits such as *attractive, educated, eloquent, friendly, hard-working, sense of humor, intelligent, polite,* and *trustworthy,* and was particularly the case for those traits that would be appealing on a personal, familiar level. The high ratings given to Belize City Kriol might be due to the fact that it comes into contact with fewer languages than Punta Gorda Kriol, leading our participants to recognize it as unmistakably Belizean "old school."

The Belize City area and the nearby villages in the Belize River valley are home to a much higher percentage of ethnic Creoles than anywhere else in the country; and, the Creoles claim Kriol as a *native* language as opposed to a second language or lingua franca as is often the case elsewhere in Belize. Many of our test participants in Punta Gorda and elsewhere in the country made comments to the effect that if we "wanted to hear real Kriol, we needed to go to Belize

[Marginal note at top: How did they get "best" from "real"]

City and to the villages." The villages in the Belize River valley can by no means be considered urban environments; thus it is interesting that there is strong agreement that these rural villages are where the best Kriol is spoken. This suggests that the lines of language prestige in coastal Belize do not necessarily run along rural-urban lines, where urban varieties are considered more prestigious and rural varieties less prestigious, as is frequently thought to be the case cross-culturally.[8] Belize City and the river valley are also predominantly monolingual, or bilingual with Kriol and English. This differs from other parts of the country, such as the south, west, and northern borders with Guatemala and Mexico, in which several languages—that is, Kriol, English, Garifuna, Spanish, and Mayan languages—are spoken side by side. The variety of Kriol spoken in the Belize City area is considered a traditional vernacular variety, as the city has a high concentration of ethnic Creoles who seldom come into contact with speakers of languages other than Kriol and English. The quantitative results clearly bear this out: Belize City Kriol is rated as more traditional than Punta Gorda Kriol, while Punta Gorda Kriol is rated as more modern than Belize City Kriol.

The conclusions we can draw from these facts fit well with the findings of many attitude surveys of creole languages reported elsewhere in the literature, in which the vernacular rates high in solidarity and personal appeal but low in power. For example, John Rickford (1985: 156), partially quoting Karl Reisman (1970: 40) on this relation, writes that "Creole [in Antigua] violates English standards of 'order, decorum, quietness, and authority,' but in which people in fact 'take great joy.'" This highly evocative description of Antiguan Creole, its formally subjugated relationship to English, and its appeal to the personal and familiar, is precisely what we found with respect to Belize City Kriol. Similar results are reported in Silvaana Udz's (2013) study of attitudes toward Kriol in primary education. In her survey of 300 schoolteachers, 87.4 percent stated that they enjoy using Kriol. Nonetheless, 47.3 percent of her participants believed that using Kriol keeps one from learning Standard English.

[Marginal note right: — It's they're active is.]

[Handwritten note at bottom: Beliefs are often misinformed.]

The Ecology of Kriol

Kriol does not exist independently of its speakers, and, as we are reminded by the seminal work of Einar Haugen (1972: 323), an analysis of Kriol is not complete without "the study of interactions between [the] given language and its environment." Drawing from principles of language ecology and especially Mufwene's (2001, 2003) analysis of creole languages in their environments, we now attend to the sociohistorical settings in which Kriol is spoken, focusing on the socioeconomic factors that largely determine its use by Belizean men and women across generations. Very little has been said about the role of gender in sociolinguistic attitudes in Belize— or the rest of the creole continuum in the Caribbean, for that matter (see Winford 1991). Escure 1991 and Salmon 2015 are exceptions, as they investigate the role of gender in linguistic variable choice and gender dialect prestige in Belize, respectively.

Great changes have taken place in these coastal sites. Placencia, where much of the fieldwork on Kriol and Garifuna reported by Escure (1981, 1991, 1997) was conducted, for example, is no longer the isolated fishing village she describes. In the last two decades the population has grown dramatically as a result of tourism, and there are many foreign-owned business and hotels, including one by the famous movie director Francis Ford Coppola. Thus, *Ocean Home: The Luxury Coastal Lifestyle Magazine* had the following to say about Placencia in May 2012: "The Placencia Peninsula, along Belize's central coastline, is the latest hotspot for Central American beachfront real estate and is home to Coppola's thatched-roof beachfront retreat, Turtle Inn. To those who've previously stumbled upon Belize's downtrodden coastal capital, Belize City, fear not; Placencia bears no resemblance to the country's economic epicenter and will quickly replace any previous feelings of 'paradise lost'" (Rubio 2012). Similarly, the Coppola Family Resorts web page for Turtle Inn promises its guests an idyllic refuge. Under the "secluded canopy of the rainforests" and "mere steps from the seashore," Coppola's guests are invited to enjoy "luxurious accommodations" and "unparalleled service" during their luxury stay.

As coastal sites like Belize City, San Pedro, Caye Caulker, and Placencia have grown as tourist destinations, the villages surrounding them have been transformed as home bases for an underclass that serves a wealthy foreign leisure tourist class. The impact on Belize's gross domestic product (GDP) has been tremendous: according to the World Travel and Tourism Council's (2017: 1) economic impact report on Belize, the total contribution of travel and tourism was 38.1 percent of GDP in 2016, and is expected to rise by 5.0 percent to 47.8 percent of GDP in 2027. The report goes on to say that the total contribution of travel and tourism to employment, including jobs indirectly supported by the industry, was 34.3 percent of Belize's total employment in 2016, and this is expected to rise to 43.2 percent of total jobs in Belize in 2027.

Over a decade and a half ago, Donna Bonner (2001: 82) wrote that "Creole speakers commonly defer to the superiority of speakers of foreign varieties of English, like those associated with the United States and England, and accord them greater prestige." In terms of overt language attitudes, foreign varieties of English are held in higher esteem, especially in formal venues. Yet our field observations over the course of four years suggest that these varieties of English might not enjoy the same prestige. More research is needed in order to further examine the linguistic hierarchy in exchanges between Belizeans and speakers of U.S., British, and Canadian English, particularly in tourist zones like Placencia and the Cayes where the largest number of cruise ships dock. Notwithstanding the presence of a linguistic hierarchy involving varieties of English, it is important to remember that financial stakeholders in Belize's tourist industry are generally citizens of North America and the United Kingdom, which already locates them in social positions of power relative to the Belizeans they employ.

Our participants often stated that Kriol should be spoken on the streets and with family but that English should be spoken in more formal settings. Yet in our ethnographic observations on university campuses in Belize and in businesses and government offices in Belize, we overheard a great deal of Kriol spoken—it wasn't spoken frequently to us, but it was certainly spoken to other speakers of Kriol. So Belizeans do speak Kriol at school and in the workplace; they just do so with other speakers of Kriol. Interestingly, in our dis-

perhaps that
is ENGLISH,

cussions with Canadian and U.S. tourists in Placencia, we learned that these groups preferred to vacation in Belize precisely for that reason: they didn't have to spend time and money learning another language (e.g., Spanish) to enjoy their vacation. And, in their eyes, both alcohol and conversation could flow freely "with the locals." These Anglophone tourists want to hear their "Belizean hosts" speaking a basilect variety of Kriol with other Belizeans, but they want their service to be provided in Standard English or an acrolectal variety of Kriol when they wish to engage in an "authentically Caribbean" experience.

The economic shift caused by the rapid growth of the tourist industry has had powerful effects on language attitudes and language use across ethnic communities in Belize. Similar to the situation documented by Walt Wolfram (2008) in his study of Okracoke Island, the economies in Belize City and Punta Gorda have transitioned steadily over the last few decades from maritime and agricultural economies that employed almost solely men to those that embrace a significant amount of international tourism, which provides advantageous economic opportunities for women in the process. As noted above, employment related to tourism in Belize accounted for over 34 percent of Belize's total employment in 2016 and is steadily growing. We do not have quantitative data on numbers of women working in the tourism sector in Belize, but based on our own experience throughout the country, women are significantly present in the hotel, restaurant, eco-, and adventure tourism business.[9] The situations of Belizeans and the Ocracoke Islanders are thus quite similar, both in the evolution of their economies and the shifting sociolinguistic attitudes of communities within them. Notably, men in both contexts indicate a strong preference for what are perceived as "traditional" varieties of the minority language, while women show a stronger affinity for varieties that showcase a greater degree of language contact at the lexical and phonological levels.[10] Taking these as points of departure, we now consider other socioeconomic factors contributing to the status of Kriol and its vitality. Two such factors are the rise of postindependence nationalism in Belize, and the large and recent waves of emigration and immigration.

Belize was one of the latest British colonies to become an independent nation. As Assad Shoman (2011) explains, "By 1961 Britain had agreed that Belize could become independent whenever it chose to; the only delay thereafter was the Guatemalan government's threat to pursue its territorial claim to Belize by force if necessary" (199). Border issues over the demarcation of British Honduras erupted between the British and Spanish crowns in the eighteenth century, and boundaries continued to be disputed even after Central America declared formal independence from Spain in 1821. Lauded as two of the most progressive Guatemalan presidents for their reforms in Guatemala, Juan José Arévalo and Jacobo Arbentz both pursued arbitration and contemplated military invasion in order to wrest away the territory they believed belonged to Guatemala. Border disputes were clearly a concern for British Honduras/Belize as it planned to claim its independence with an intact territory, and this created a tense relationship between the colony and its colonial officials, who pointed to the costs of protecting British Honduras/Belize. One official declared in 1962:

> British Honduras is an embarrassment to Her Majesty's Government, both [*sic*] politically, militarily and financially. Politically, it is anachronistic to maintain a colony on the American continent in the 1960s: its existence complicates Her Majesty's Governments' relations with all the Latin American States. . . . Militarily, the maintenance of the garrison in British Honduras is a commitment which we ought to shed as soon as possible. Financially, British Honduras costs Her Majesty's government half a million pounds per annum simply to balance the budget. Added to these general disadvantages is our long-standing dispute with Guatemala, which is costing us about 1 million pounds per annum in lost trade already, and if the Guatemalan government decides to break relations with us, could lead to the loss of substantial assets as well. (qtd. in Shoman 2011: 213–14)

Through the 1960s and 1970s, threats of invasion and attempts at negotiation continued. Even as war and genocide erupted in Central America around British Honduras/Belize, plans for its independence moved forward. Belize gained international support, set a date for its independence, and, most important, Britain made preparations to remain in Belize "for an appropriate period" to defend it against any possible Guatemalan invasion. The British remained in the country from 1981 to 1993. So long as British forces continued to defend an independent Belize and the United States was in full accord with the agreement, Guatemala could not invade the youngest nation in Central America without causing severe diplomatic tensions. However, far from being a thing of the past, border disputes with Guatemala continue to this day.

Many of the Belizeans we spoke with in our research—those roughly in their forties today—would have been children and young adults when Belize gained its independence in 1981. Raised in one of the most dramatic socioeconomic shifts ever experienced in Belize, their eyes would have been wide open as their country became what Shoman (2011: 331) calls "a dependent (independent) Belize in the world economy." They experienced the transition from colonial economy to postmodern economy, and *chose* to remain in Belize to see it through. By remaining in the young country, they became part of the process of Belizean nation-making and ethnolinguistic identity-making.

Shoman observes that although colonialism had ended, the colonial mentality and dominant culture weighed heavily on Belize as it worked to define itself. Even with the relocation of the national government from Belize City to Belmopan, the English colonial presence continued to have important cultural symbolism. Past and present came together as the new nation was imagined as Creole: "People that spoke English, were Anglicized in other cultural ways, and practiced a unique 'Belizean way of life,' which could be interpreted best by members of the Creole elite. True, other members of the nation were tolerated and even celebrated as folkloric manifestations that made Belize interesting and quaint, but the bedrock of the nation was a British inheritance, 'those institutions, laws and high principles characteristic of the Anglo-Saxons' that the 1951 Creole constitutional commissions had spoken of" (Shoman 2011: 360). Creating a sense of place and rightful belonging was predicated on the way Belizeans would frame their national identity in the present (in museums, the Central Bank, the courts) and imagine the past (in national myths, colonial history, the Westminster system), as well as on a collective national imaginary with respect to ethnicity and identity politics (Sutherland 1998: 60). Debates about Creole culture—and at the root of this, the Kriol language—are an integral part of the process. As McClaurin (1996: 2) observes, "Rather than Creole culture being taken as another example of cultural diffusion, innovation and transculturation in the Americas, the lingering evidence of British tastes in food, manners, daily routines (like tea time), and education" remains in Creole culture.

Accelerated change in Belize has been the rule of the day since 1981, but as Mara Voorhees and Joshua Brown put it in the 2008 *Lonely Planet: Belize* tourist guidebook, "Kriol is *di stikki stikki paat* that holds Belize together." This is perhaps evermore true in the context of the emigration flows that have forever altered the demographics of the small country. Writing in 2007, Jerome Straughan estimated that there were then between 110,000 and 120,000 Belizeans living in the United States, and that 30 percent of the Belizean American population was born in the United States. This migratory flow out of Belize was about 75 percent Creole and Garifuna, both with African roots, leading to a decrease in the number of ethnic Creoles in Belize. At the same time, Belize experienced a significant wave of immigration driven by the conflict and genocide in neighboring Guatemala, Honduras, and El Salvador in the 1980s. The population of Belize was 145,000 in 1980, and by 1985 it was estimated that up to 30,000 new Central American immigrants had arrived. According to the 1990 Belize census, Creoles comprised 30 percent of the population, compared with 40 percent in 1980, and Mestizos became 44 percent of the population, compared with 33 percent in 1980. The 2000 Belize census counted ethnic Creoles at 25 percent of the population and Mestizo at 48 percent. The number of Mestizos in Belize, however, is a complex matter since the figure collapses groups of people with a long-standing presence in Belize (that is, those fleeing the Caste War of Yucatán in the late nineteenth century) with more recent Spanish-speaking Central American immigrants and their children, who were born on Beli-

TABLE 1. Ratings of Belize City Kriol and Punta Gorda Kriol by age cohort

	BC Kriol	Significant differences	PG Kriol
All 18–34			
Status	3.25	$F = 5.55, p = .018$	3.05
Solidarity	3.81	$F = 21.16, p = <.0001$	3.43
All 35–60			
Status	3.49	$F = 16, p = <.0001$	3.10
Solidarity	3.78	$F = 31.1, p = <.0001$	3.26

zean soil and speak Kriol with as much ease as any other Belizean of their generation.

Both emigration and immigration have caused a demographic shift of dramatic proportions, and, we observe, have thrown linguistic and cultural differences into sharp relief. Creole-speaking Belizeans of all ethnicities and Spanish-speaking immigrants of different Central American nationalities compete for resources and employment, even as multimillion-dollar resorts are built in their small villages with U.S. and Canadian capital. In the midst of this, identifying with a Creole culture and speaking Kriol, both products of a colonial past that anteceded flight *from* Belize and flight *to* Belize, become indicators of belongingness that mark speakers as true Belizeans. In our study, we found an overall appreciation for two different varieties of Belizean Kriol across generations. Both regional language varieties (that is, Kriol as spoken in Belize City and as spoken in Punta Gorda) were ranked quite favorably among all groups; however, the Belize City variety was ranked significantly higher in status and solidarity traits, as shown in table 1, where the group aged 18–34 rated Belize City Kriol significantly higher than Punta Gorda Kriol, as did the group aged 35–60.[11] When we compared the 18–34 group from Belize City with the 18–34 group from Punta Gorda, we found no significant differences in how the varieties were rated. This suggests that the young people of coastal Belize, who were born and came of age after independence in 1981, are very alike in their attitudes toward both varieties of Kriol, seeing both varieties as instances of the national language.

The same was not true for the older age group when we compared results from Belize City and Punta Gorda. Our older participants—those who were teenagers when Belize became an independent nation and who saw Belize City through its many transformations—show a significantly stronger preference for Belize City Kriol, regardless of their place of residence. This suggests that Belize City Kriol has long been considered the standard or "best" variety, and our many interviews around the country confirmed this perception.

It is only with the younger, post-independence speakers that the elevation of the Kriol language in general has occurred. Clearly, Belize City Kriol has grown to symbolize a fresh national identity, at once emblematic of a colonial past without being subject to it, and thus more "authentically Belizean" and prestigious than any of the other languages spoken in the country. At the same time, especially with the younger generations, other varieties of Kriol are not displeasing to the Belizean ear, and they symbolize a national Belizean identity as well, if to a slightly lesser extent.

Linguistic Belonging

The two popular sayings—"Belize is for Belizeans" and "Dis da fi wi langwij"—bring to bear the connections between nation, national identity, and linguistic belonging. As Robert Le Page and Andrée Tabouret-Keller (1985) note in their seminal work on creole languages in Cayo District in 1978, the term *Belizean* designated a citizen of the soon-to-be independent nation of Belize, and had a very strong connotation with the use of Kriol. Ethnic identification, strongly linked to community and geographical location, had given way to a sense of belonging to an independent country. British Honduran no longer, national identity began to override local conceptualizations of identity: "Those who had formerly had an identity as 'Spanish,' or 'Carib,' or 'Maya,' or 'Kekchi,' or 'Waika' (a somewhat denigratory term in common use for the Miskito) or Lebanese or 'Creole,' and as British colonial subjects would now, if they chose to stay in the country, have to find an identity within the new state" (117). For many young Belizeans, the transition meant that their identities would then be predicated on the basis of something other than the language spoken in their communities (221). As Le Page and Tabouret-Keller noted then, in most cases where Belizean identity was mentioned, Kriol was spoken of as "the Belizean language" (220). This in Cayo District, which they conceptualized as "a rather empty buffer zone between the coastal Creoles of the Belize district and the Spanish, Maya and Mestizos of Guatemala who had spilled over as political refugees to establish the small town of Benque Viejo" (217). We have discovered that this is *now* also true of Mayan and Garifuna communities in the coastal districts of Belize.

The sociopolitical changes from 1981 to the present have allowed all Belizeans, and members of these communities in particular, to declare a linguistic identity that is more closely associated with citizenship and belongingness in the new nation than with their village affiliation. The implications of this change are important to bear in mind as we move forward in our analysis of the factors that contribute to the use and endangerment of minority languages in Belize. Similarly, it is important to note that Kriol works as an identity marker that allows speakers to identify themselves as citizens of Belize, and to distinguish "true" Belizeans from non-Belizeans. The socioeconomic changes that Belize has undergone in the last thirty-five years have left their mark on the cultural and environmental landscape—the rise of the tourist sector, the designation of Belizean land for the purpose of natural reserves, the sale of land to foreign companies and investors, as well as emigration and immigration have created a country that is very much in flux. Throughout this complex demographic shift, the Kriol language appears to have a long future as the most salient marker of Belizean identity.

In addition to the historically advantageous position of Kriol, there has been a strong language revitalization movement headed by the Belize Kriol Project and National Kriol Council of Belize, which aims to promote the language. The group has targeted educational institutions as the focus of change, especially primary schools in response to the country's official educational policy (see Ministry of Education 2008; and Udz 2013). They have also been at the forefront of establishing a writing system for Kriol that has been met with a mixed reception—with some enthusiastic support but also strong opposition—as opponents claim that developing a writing system seeks to legitimize a flawed and broken language.[12]

Outside of the educational realm, the Belize Kriol Project and the National Kriol Council of Belize have spearheaded notable projects, such as an English/Kriol dictionary published in 2007 and a Kriol translation of *The New Testament*, which appeared in print in 2013 and can now be read in its entirety online.[13] These projects complement a postindependence literary movement launched with the publication of Zee Edgell's *Beka Lamb* (1982) and Glen Godfrey's *The Sinner's Bossanova* (1987). These were the precursors of a movement that sought to establish a national Belizean literary tradition, founded on the language and themes of its people, and have been followed by a succession of writers and poets for whom Kriol is a central feature of their work (Ruiz Puga 2001).[14] As of this writing, the often hotly debated Kriol appears in books, magazines, advertisements, and newspapers. It is also found on the radio and in cyberspace, and it has been the subject of linguistic analyses, which include, most notably, linguistic grammars such as Young 1973, Greene 1999, and Decker 2005. Despite the misconceptions and overt negative attitudes about Kriol, the language plays an important role in mass media and advertising, particularly in relation to the tourist industry. Taking these factors into account, Kriol occupies an undeniably visible place in Belizean society that no other language in the country is positioned to hold. It possesses an irrefutable vitality, even as its native speakers discredit its linguistic value. As we will show in the remaining chapters, despite this seeming contradictory set of positions, Kriol appears to be having strong effects on other minority languages in the country.

Chapter Three

Mopan

Between Tradition and Change

The 1798 Battle of St. George's Caye, in which the British and their slaves purportedly stood shoulder-to-shoulder to defeat the Spanish, has become immortalized as a founding myth, passed down to generations of Belizeans in grade schools across the country (Moberg 1997). This origin myth even gave rise to the Kriol saying, "We da fu ya, everybody else da come ya," which crystallized the sentiment that other ethnic groups were newcomers and outsiders (Bolland and Moberg 1995; Shoman 2011). Ethnohistorical evidence demonstrates, however, that Mayan groups have maintained a continuous presence in Belize for centuries, with the earliest Mopan communities located in central and northern Belize, where the closely related Yucatec language and culture flourished historically (Wilk and Chapin 1990; Moberg 1997; Jones 1989).[1]

Many of the Mopan communities in Belize were destroyed or uprooted by the Spanish over the course of the sixteenth, seventeenth, and eighteenth centuries. In 1886, however, a Mopan group from San Luis, Guatemala, themselves fleeing persecution and enslavement, relocated to southern Belize, founding the village of present-day San Antonio (Sapper 1897: 54; Thompson 1930: 41; Bolland 1988: 206).[2] Though a few other Mopan settlements were established in Cayo District around the same time, these communities soon lost much of their Mopan identity through intermarriage with Yucatec or Mestizo outsiders (Wilk and Chapin 1990: 12). In contrast, Nigel Bolland (1988: 206) observes, those who settled in the isolated villages of Toledo maintained a strong sense of identity, language, dress, and religion as a result of the economic and cultural isolation. As one colonial official wrote in 1887, "The Indians [Maya] were scattered about in small villages, the access to which was most difficult, so that no control was really exercised over them" (qtd. in Shoman 2011: 111). The extreme isolation of the Mopan in Toledo remained virtually unchanged until the Toledo Maya Cultural Council was formed in 1978 to address the needs and claim the rights of Mayas in the district (Toledo Maya Cultural Council 1997: 3). As we discuss in the present chapter, this economic and national integration has subsequently played a direct role in the diminishing state of the Mopan language.

Setting the Stage for Fieldwork

Mopan belongs to the Yucatecan branch of the Mayan language family, which also includes Yucatec, Lacandón, and Itzá. The first two are primarily spoken in Mexico, with Yucatec having a healthy 800,000 speakers and Lacandón seriously endangered with approximately 1,000 speakers. Itzá and Mopan are spoken in Guatemala, and are considered endangered there as well.[3] Speakers of Mayan languages in Mexico and Guatemala have been subject to a process of *castellanización* that parallels the experiences of indigenous languages in other former Spanish colonies. Across the border in Belize, however, Mayans have been subjected to a complex process of Anglicization experienced by British subjects and now, members of the Commonwealth.

According to the 2010 Belize census, there were 30,478 speakers of Mayan languages in Belize, of which 68 percent lived in Toledo District and another 16.3 percent lived in Stann Creek District. At 10,649 speakers, Mopan was the second-largest Mayan linguistic group in the country (there were 17,586 speakers of Kekchi and 2,518 speakers of Yucatec). This only apparently healthy figure conceals an important fact, however: between 1980 and 2010 the number of Mopan speakers decreased 3.6 percent while the number of Kekchi speakers rose 6 percent (Tanaka-Farlane 2015). Yuki Tanaka (2012) appears to be the first researcher to focus primarily on the endangerment of the Mopan language, while tangential discussion of this concern also arises in Salmon and Gómez Menjívar 2016. For that matter, there has been limited interest in the grammar and use of Mopan in general, with key exceptions found in Danziger 1996, 2001; Hofling 2011; and Kaufman and Justeson 2003, which have explored various aspects of Mopan grammar.[4]

Toledo District, home to most members of the Mopan community, has been known as the "forgotten district" for several years, and its socioeconomic differences from Belize District are striking. For example, Belize District has the largest urban population (72 percent), while Toledo has the smallest urban population (17 percent). Furthermore, 88 percent of the working-age population in Belize District has completed at least primary school education, compared to 58 percent in Toledo. Belize District has the highest rate of Internet usage, at 38 percent, while Toledo has the lowest, at 16 percent. Homeownership was higher in Toledo, but the homes in the two districts were very different: 24 percent of the homes in Toledo had earth/sand as the main flooring material (compared to 0.2 percent of the homes in Belize District), 48 percent of the inhabitants in Toledo used wood/coal as their primary cooking fuel (compared to 2 percent of the homes in Belize District).[5] While the tourist industry has historically created a wider array of professional opportunities for the inhabitants of Belize District, few such options were available to inhabitants of Toledo until the 1990s, when eco- and cultural tourism began to be pursued by the district's Mayan communities.[6] Given the wide-ranging socioeconomic and linguistic variation between the two districts, we expected to find significant differences in attitudes toward Mopan and Kriol as well.

In order to gauge attitudes toward Mopan, we conducted a preliminary survey on the streets of Punta Gorda and Belize City, which included questions such as the following:

(a) Have you heard of the Mopan language spoken in Belize?
(b) Should Mopan be taught in Belizean schools?
(c) Should the Belizean government protect the Mopan language?
(d) Should the Belizean government protect any language spoken in Belize?

We surmised that the multilingual context of Punta Gorda would lead participants to express stronger positive opinions about language policy for Mopan specifically, and for the languages of Belize in general. We spoke with a total of forty Belizeans, evenly divided between Punta Gorda and Belize City. Our closed questions very often resulted in further conversation with the individuals we queried in Punta Gorda, though we observed this was not the case in Belize City.

More participants in Punta Gorda (PG) than Belize City (BC) had heard of the Mopan language, as was expected (PG 89 percent, BC 75 percent). Surprisingly, participants in Punta Gorda were less likely to support the teaching of Mopan in schools (PG 47 percent, BC 85 percent). One Garifuna male in his twenties stated that it was impractical, while a Kekchi man in his sixties stated that it should only be taught at the vocational level and not necessarily to everyone. Participants in Punta Gorda were also less likely to indicate that the Belizean government should protect Mopan (PG 68 percent, BC 85 percent). Another Kekchi man in his sixties stated, for example, that the government should "protect the people, not the language." Our last question received high affirmative responses (PG 84 percent, BC 95 percent), and the open nature of this question resulted in the greatest number of comments. For example, two Creole men in their thirties stated that all languages should be protected, while a Mestizo teacher in his forties stated that Spanish and English should be protected; a Garifuna woman in her sixties stated that all should be protected, as "God gave us language." These results indicated favorable attitudes toward linguistic diversity in general, but mixed reactions toward protecting Mopan in particular. We therefore decided to look further into the state of Mopan, its place in Toledo District and in Belize.

Fieldwork in San Antonio

San Antonio is located in the foothills of the Maya Mountains and is widely considered to be the cultural home of the Mopan in Belize (map 2). There are roughly 800 residents in San Antonio, and it is by most accounts the last remaining Belizean village in which Mopan is the primary language. Other Mopan villages in Belize have large percentages of Kekchi and Spanish-speaking in-

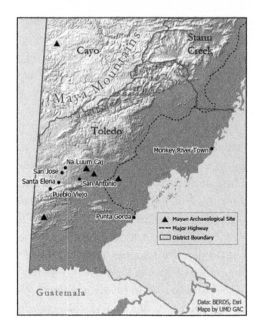

Map 2. Toledo District, Belize. Courtesy of the UMD Geospatial Analysis Center, Map data BERDS, Esri.

habitants, as intermarriages have become increasingly common (Tanaka 2012, Tanaka-McFarlane 2015). Upon our arrival we met with one of the village elders and shared our observations about Kriol and our interest in the Mopan language. At his suggestion, we then met with the leader of San Antonio and obtained permission to query the community about language use.

We collected seventy-eight quantitative surveys in the community from forty women and thirty-eight men (approximately 10 percent of San Antonio's inhabitants), ages twelve to seventy-eight. A female native speaker of Mopan who lives in the village administered the surveys in peer fashion, introducing the survey and its goals to participants who often completed them as a family. She also assisted in translating questions for participants when appropriate. The surveys included demographic questions, statements regarding the Mopan language specifically, and statements concerning Mopan vis-à-vis English or Kriol depending on which survey participants had received. There were no other differences in the structure of the two surveys except for the inclusion of English or Kriol in the relevant statements. Statements regarding the Mopan language (e.g., "One cannot be considered Mopan if one does not speak Mopan") and statements involving English or Kriol (e.g., "I would like Mopan to replace English as a medium of instruction in our public schools" or "My ability to speak Kriol will assure me a good job as soon as I finish school") were arranged on a Likert scale, with 1 designating "strongly disagree" and 5 designating "strongly agree."

Our participants from San Antonio village were quite uniform in socioeconomic status: 77 percent of our participants listed their father's occupation as "farmer," while 91 percent listed their mother's occupation as "housewife." All but two of our participants chose Mopan as their ethnic identification, while one identified as Mopan/East Indian and another as Kekchi/East Indian. The linguistic background of our participants ran parallel to their ethnic identifications: when asked which language they learned as a baby, 95 percent answered Mopan; 2.5 percent answered Kriol; 1.3 percent Mopan/East Indian;[7] and 1.3 percent Kekchi/East Indian. Nonetheless, 95 percent of participants stated that they spoke Mopan well or very well. Notably, the 5 percent who said they spoke Mopan "not well" were not among those who indicated Kriol as their first language. These responses tell us less about proficiency itself and more about strong positive attitudes toward the language and target culture.[8] Older participants tended to indicate that they were bilingual (Mopan and English), while younger participants tended to indicate that they were multilingual and spoke several languages, including Mopan, Kekchi, English, Kriol, and Spanish, "very well."

Overt attitudes toward English and Kriol were largely predictable. Statements such as "My ability to speak ____ will assure me a good job as soon as I finish school," "My ability to speak ____ is a matter of pride for my parents," and "My ability to speak ____ will assure my success in the future" received higher ratings when referring to English rather than Kriol, with no significant differences found when we controlled for sex or age. There were also no significant differences relating to the implementation of Mopan instead of English in primary, secondary, and tertiary education. There were, however, significant differences between younger and older participants when asked if Mopan should replace Kriol in these educational environments. Surprisingly, the surveys that contained questions about Kriol had an impact on how participants answered queries about Mopan identity—even when those queries made no mention of another ethnicity. For example, the statement "One cannot be considered Mopan if one does not speak Mopan," gathered very different results depending on whether the language foregrounded in the survey was English or Kriol.[9] Essentially, younger and older participants agreed about the relation between Mopan language and identity when the comparison language was English. In contrast, there was much less agreement between the younger and older groups when the comparison language was Kriol. This suggests that with respect to Mopan, the Kriol language is rising in prestige or desirability among the younger generation, while the relationship between Mopan and English is much more static.

We found similar dynamics across a range of other linguistic comparisons involving the three languages. In each comparison, the results show an elevation in the desirability of Kriol with respect to Mopan. These responses thus shed light on covert attitudes toward the Mopan language that are quite distinct for younger and older generations.

At a Distance, in Punta Gorda

The second phase of our study took place in Punta Gorda, which is located thirty kilometers (18.6 miles) southeast of San Antonio on the coast. Punta Gorda is one of the most ethnically diverse towns in Belize. The population is composed primarily of ethnic Creoles, Garinagus, Kekchi and Mopan Mayas, East Indians, and Chinese Belizeans in addition to immigrants from neighboring El Salvador, Guatemala, and Honduras. While many inhabitants speak their respective languages with other members of their group, the language used to communicate across groups is Kriol. Indeed, it is common to see Mennonite customers bargaining in the market in Kriol with a Mayan or Mestizo woman. Punta Gorda is accessible by car and bus, and daily flights arrive from Belize City. Nonetheless, its lack of beaches has led this coastal town to develop an inland tourist industry, highlighting the Mayan archaeological sites of Toledo District shown in map 2, above.

While bed and breakfast–style lodgings and restaurants can be found on the waterfront, an elementary school, churches, stalls on market days, town-center shops, and a fish market are all on the same coastal strip. Aside from the Fajina Mayan Crafts Center and the Warasa Garifuna Drumming School, few businesses draw a primarily tourist clientele. With the growth of cultural and ecotourism concentrated inland, the development of foreign-owned Mayan-themed resorts and ecolodges is occurring outside of the city limits proper. Punta Gorda itself is, at this time, a residential area that primarily serves the needs of its inhabitants.

The Mayan participants for this phase of the study were a subset of those interviewed in our study on attitudes toward Kriol described in chapter 2. This included thirty-eight participants in Punta Gorda who identified as Mopan Mayan, Kekchi Mayan, or Mopan-Kekchi Mayan. Strikingly, our quantitative results indicated that Mayas as a subset rated Kriol higher across all categories than all the other ethnic groups combined. Furthermore, all of the Mayas in this subset were college students and provided us with substantial anecdotes to warrant consideration of the place of Kriol and Mayan languages in their lives.

On our surveys, Mayan students responded that Kriol was spoken with friends, at home, in Belize City, and in Punta Gorda. We observed a high degree of bilingualism during our conversations with them and as they completed their surveys.[10] Participants typically didn't speak Kriol to us directly, but it was certainly the language they used with their friends as they joked and teased each other about who finished the quickest and who guessed the "correct" origin of the speakers. Outside of these spontaneous "focus groups," we observed Kriol spoken between Mayan friends while they chatted outside their classrooms and on the grounds of the campus. Although more research is needed in this particular area, our sense was that the young Mayas we observed in the test situation and ethnographic setting moved with ease in the mesolectal area on

TABLE 2. Variational points along the Kriol continuum

Variational point	Example
Basilect	Di flai dehn mi-di bait laas nait.
Mesolect	Di flies dem mi bitin las nite.
	Dem flayz de baytin las nait.
	Di flayz-dem de waz baytin.
Acrolect	Di mosquitos were bitin las nite.
Standard English	The mosquitos were biting last night.

the Kriol continuum (table 2).[11] We surmise from their responses to our surveys and the linguistic behavior we observed, that many young Mayas in Belize speak Kriol in informal situations and with each other, both inside and outside of their Mayan villages. This is interesting, as we did not observe young Mayas speaking Garifuna or Spanish among each other. This suggests that even though these other local languages are spoken in the same geographic space, only Kriol has emerged as a language with added value.

This appears to be especially true for the newest generation of Belizean Mayas, those whose childhoods were spent post-1981 in the newly independent country. Unlike their parents, the vast majority of whom are farmers depending on subsistence agrarian economies, or their mothers who became housewives and depended on their husbands as breadwinners, they have gained access to higher education, a wider range of employment opportunities, and have become better integrated in the social fabric of the country. Speaking Kriol provides the younger generation with a comparative advantage that is unmatched by any other language spoken in Toledo District, and it is useful in postindependence Belize in a way that it was not for older Mayas when they were in their twenties. Educational success is important in Mayan families, just as serving the community is an important value that elders expect children to uphold. As the *Maya Atlas* written by the Toledo Maya Cultural Council (1997: 134) states, "Some young Mayans get opportunities for higher education beyond the primary level. These young people are considered elites in their villages." Both in our conversations with elders in San Antonio and in our conversations with members of younger generations, we heard stories about young Mopan returning to the village to serve as teachers and cultural workers, occupying positions in small nongovernmental organizations and cultural centers. Yet despite the pervasive belief across the country that Kriol is broken English, acrolectal and mesolectal Kriol provides young speakers of the language an option that can be beneficial, particularly if the positions they seek are in the emerging tourist industry in Toledo District.

Kriol is an integral part of the daily lives of these young Mayas, while Spanish is useful in other areas of the country but less beneficial closer to home. In Toledo District, Kriol offers promises of upward mobility and sufficient models to attest to the connection between language and career advancement. Meanwhile, the Spanish speakers we encountered in Toledo were almost uniformly immigrants in low-wage occupations. The only monolingual Spanish speaker we met in San Antonio worked as a cook for a Mopan couple who owned a restaurant and spoke English and Mopan with a degree of difficulty. In Punta Gorda, the Spanish speakers we met worked as vendors, though not owners, in shops in the downtown area. Like the newly arrived Chinese in Punta Gorda, monolingual Spanish speakers live a world apart from Belizeans of all ethnic groups in Toledo.[12] We heard no Spanish in the courtyard of the campus, none between the groups of Mayan friends waiting outside of class, and none during our "focus groups" with Mayan participants. The responses to our question about where it was appropriate to speak Spanish reflected this Spanishless context. "Spanish sites" were outside of our participants' immediate circle of Mayan friends and beyond their Mayan and Punta Gorda communities. This might be related to the status of Spanish observed elsewhere in Belize, especially Orange Walk District, where it is negatively perceived even among native speakers of Spanish (Balam and Prada Pérez 2017). We suspect further that Spanish in Punta Gorda has an even higher stigmatization due to the proximity of Livingston, Guatemala, at a distance of just 19.2 nautical miles, and the ongoing threat of annexation to the Guatemalan territory. Furthermore, as we have written elsewhere and as other scholars have stated before us, there remains a negative attitude toward immigration from other Central American nations to Belize.

The Place of Mopan in Toledo ... the Place of Mopan in Belize

There are important socioeconomic reasons for speakers of Mopan to also speak English. Speaking the official language of the country opens doors to higher education and the professions, making it possible to achieve a higher standard of living than the previous generation. As the tourist industry begins to move deeper into Toledo District, young Mayas who have attended college are also faced with the choice of remaining in their rural communities or leaving to pursue job opportunities in Punta Gorda, or further away to Belize City or off the coast to the islands, where individuals who are hired in higher-level professions are expected to have a high command of Standard English and, concurrently, an acrolectal variety of Kriol. Thus, at the same time that younger Mopan view Kriol as the language of friendship and of recreation used outside of the village context, Kriol is also taking on the added value of socioeconomic usefulness. This stands in stark opposition to our younger participants' perception of Mopan as a more traditional language and one more likely to be spoken in the village or over the phone with parents and grandparents. It is almost a mirror image of their elders' perception of Kriol as a language spoken by a specific ethnic group in another district a world away.

Belize's international reputation as an all-inclusive, diverse, and friendly country has origins in the independence movement. Indeed, one of the movement's important projects was to bring Belize's ethnic communities into the fold by instilling in them a sense of pride in the new nation.[13] Belize's first history textbook stated: "Our population is made up of Creoles, Mestizos, Garifuna, Maya, Mennonites; and people with Arab, East Indian, Chinese, European, British or other ancestry, and any number of combinations. Each group brings with it a rich heritage and helps to make our national culture" (Nembhard 1990: 18). Thirty-six years after independence, young Belizeans continue to be taught to appreciate the rich cultural and ethnic diversity of their nation through Belizean history lessons and cultural festivals celebrated annually throughout the country. Educational policy and positive attitudes, however, are not enough to secure linguistic vitality. Intergenerational transmission of a language is the most important indicator of language maintenance, since only when intergenerational transmission of a language ceases can it be said that speakers have shifted to another language (Fishman 1991). Kriol has already become the first language of the youngest members of the San Antonio Mopan community, while Kekchi continues to be the first language of many young people born in mixed Mopan-Kekchi households outside of San Antonio.[14] The appeal of another Mayan language is easily explained, as Mayan kinship networks remain paramount to individuals across generations. However, the appeal of Kriol is relatively new and quite striking, since it reveals a turn to a language that appears at first blush to be on equal footing to Mopan as a minority language.[15]

The literature on language endangerment has long focused on language endangerment as a product of the core-periphery relationship between the global North and global South and the repercussions of this relationship on local languages outside of Europe and North America. We must nonetheless remember that, "at a more local scale, almost every country has its cores and peripheries, and at the boundaries of almost all these, peripheral languages are on the retreat" (Nettle and Romaine 2000: 209). Our study concurs with the linguistic literature in the field that the driving force of this retreat is not personal or even interpersonal but macro- and micro-economic. After all, what determines the peripherality of a language is not the language itself but the differences in the economies and societies of the people who speak it. Seen in this light, language shift occurs when linguistic communities in contact "have radically different economic roles: not equal like two groups of forest foragers, and not complementary, like a coastal gatherer meeting an island hunter, but in which the prospects of one party are a superset of the prospects of the other" (Nettle and Romaine 2000: 130). Although derived from a binary understanding of languages in competition for prominence, the observation is useful for understanding the divergent economic roles of English, Kriol, and Mopan within a single context—in this case, Toledo District. As English, Kriol, and Mopan assume different positions in the economic future of Belizean Mayas, the economic utility of these languages are reevaluated by their speakers.

Our results suggest that an important change in the ecology of Mopan is that Kriol, along with English, is a formidable competitor in the linguistic landscape. Although the Mopan/non-Mopan "boundary" was breached in the 1930s, when the road between San Antonio and Punta Gorda was first built, as late as 1976 contact between speakers of Mopan and outsiders was largely limited to economic transactions taking place during brief visits to the town (Gregory 1976). With the outsiders' cultural influence so minimal, the process of linguistic creolization that had spread from Belize District to other districts—Cayo, Orange Walk, and Corozal—had not occurred in Toledo District until this present generation. The Mopan-English bilingualism of the older generation is no longer enough to ensure the economic stability of families and the larger Mopan community; younger Mayas today need Kriol to ensure the economic viability of their kinship networks.

As linguistic research has demonstrated repeatedly, language maintenance depends on many factors, including a community's degree of isolation and/or urbanization, emigration, and cyclical migration; the size of the linguistic community; formal and informal opportunities for speakers to use the language, including its use at home and in religious and educational institutions; and whether or not it is transmitted to future generations (Montrul 2012). Isolation is clearly undesirable, particularly in light of the territorial issues that Mayan communities in Toledo continue to face and for which solidarity and support across ethnic lines is needed.[16] At the same time, however, integration into the national fold is clearly a threat to Mayan cultural identity in its own way. Yet emigration and urbanization do not have to claim speakers of Mopan languages in the process. As has been observed in the cases of Mayan communities in Guatemala, maintaining ties to the homeland, to elders, and to spiritual ceremonies is paramount in cultural and linguistic maintenance. In the case of the Mopan language in Belize, a foundation for that appears to be in place already, as cultural pride was seen to be quite strong among our participants. Whether this is enough to ensure the language's survival remains to be seen.

Languages, of course, have neither birth nor death certificates, but we can track the process of language atrophy—and the reverse process of language maintenance—as the number of situations in which a language can be used diminishes or rises (Mufwene 2006). At present, the growth of sites responding to exponential increases in tourism is drawing the youngest members of Mayan communities away from their rural hometowns and traditional agricultural livelihoods.[17] The loss of assets, in the form of both territory and speakers, is experienced in conjunction with the advancement of tourism in this landscape. So long as the process proceeds in a manner that obstructs Mayan sovereignty over ancestral lands and their natural resources, the situation will quickly reduce the number of contexts in which speakers of Mopan, and other Mayan languages, perceive their language as cultural capital.[18] What evidence will speakers use to determine the usefulness of their language as arguments over ancestral land rights are heard in the courts, and what will the place of Mopan be if the forests, rivers, and waterfalls where it is spoken are no longer settings for its use? The effects of the wave of socioeconomic transition on this community are already audible in this tropical scenery.

Chapter Four

Garifuna

An Ethnolinguistic Identity in Flux

The story of the Garifuna communities of coastal Belize is fraught with hardship, migration, and contact with other peoples as the Garifuna moved through various points in the Caribbean and Central America before landing in Belize. Garifuna peoples are believed to have descended from the intermarriage of African slaves with indigenous Amerindian Caribs in the Caribbean, and the contemporary Garifuna language reflects this history as well as the extensive contact with European colonizers in the region. As Escure (2004: 36) notes, the language "has been claimed to have a primary Arawak substrate, combined with other linguistic elements, including Carib, Spanish, French and English."[1] Over the centuries, Arawakan languages were brought to Central America and the Caribbean through migration; yet Garifuna is the only Arawakan language spoken in the region today. Sometime prior to the 1600s, the Arawak peoples on the island of St. Vincent were conquered or absorbed by an indigenous Carib group. The resulting linguistic blend of Cariban and Arawakan languages was what was found on St. Vincent in the 1600s when the shipwrecked African slaves arrived, and remnants of both Cariban and Arawakan languages are well represented in the Garifuna language today. According to Escure (2004: 46), the grammar of Garifuna appears "to include synthetic Arawakan morphosyntax, as well as lexical and morphological Carib elements."

Garifuna history prior to 1797 is not clear; however, it is accepted by many historians and the Garifuna themselves that the genesis of the Garifuna people occurred sometime in the 1600s, when two Spanish ships carrying African slaves to the Caribbean were shipwrecked near St. Vincent.[2] The surviving Africans who made it ashore then mixed with the indigenous Carib-Arawak population on the island, and over several generations they came to be known as "Black Caribs."[3] In 1797, the Black Caribs were forcibly removed from St. Vincent by the British and mostly relocated to Roatan Island off the coast of Honduras.[4] Farming conditions on Roatan were much less amenable than on St. Vincent, and members of the group very soon moved to mainland Honduras and shortly thereafter began migrating northward to coastal Belize. By the mid-late nineteenth century, groups of Black Caribs had established several communities in Belize, including the village of Seine Bight, which provides the case study for the present work.

Belizean Garifuna Communities Today

When Belize gained its independence from the United Kingdom in 1981, the Garifuna gained official recognition, and as Escure notes, "*Black Carib* gave way to *Garifuna* (and *Garinagu*) as a sign of respect." There are several Garifuna communities in Belize today, and they make up approximately 6 percent of the nation's population, with roughly 19,000 people claiming Garifuna ethnicity around the country (Statistical Institute of Belize 2010).[5] The primary Garifuna communities in Belize are found in the towns of Dangriga and Punta Gorda and the smaller villages of Seine Bight, Hopkins, Barranco, and Georgetown. The last two Garifuna communities listed, Barranco and Georgetown, are small and are commonly represented as having aging populations with little presence of Garifuna youth who speak the language. The Garifuna community in Punta Gorda is substantially larger than those of the aforementioned communities; yet in Punta Gorda, an extremely diverse town of Creoles, Mayans, East Indians, Chinese, Mennonites, and Mestizos, one likewise hears very little Garifuna on the street.[6]

Dangriga, in Stann Creek District, is commonly considered to be the cultural capital of the Garifuna people: the largest Garifuna population is located there, and it is home to the National Garifuna Council, the Gulisi Garifuna Museum, and a bilingual English/Garifuna primary school.[7] Yet, even in Dangriga the Garifuna language occupies a precarious space. Bonner (2001: 94), for example, relays a poignant story of a Dangriga woman in her late thirties who spoke Garifuna around town as an act of defiance, and who was written off as "crazy" by many in the town. The narrative is worth repeating here:

> I never once heard her speak a word of Creole or Spanish. She would walk into the store where we both shopped and give her order to the Creole store-owner, speaking "lone Garifuna" in a voice loud enough to carry out the windows and into the neighbors' yards. The owner waited on her, a scowl on his face, handing her everything she requested. He had learned Garifuna twenty years earlier, when he was a small boy and his family had first moved from Creole-dominated Belize City to Dangriga to open a grocery store. At that time, Garifuna was unquestionably the language of Dangriga, and those who owned businesses in town had to learn it. This is no longer true. Dangriga is no longer simply the Garifuna town of Belize. It is, rather, a multiethnic Belizean town. Furthermore, in the context of immigration from Spanish-speaking countries, the language that authentic Belizeans are expected to speak is English Creole. Today, this woman's use of Garifuna is an act of resistance; when coupled with the broader social context, it is dismissed as "crazy."

This story from Dangriga could be generalized to most of the Garifuna communities in Belize. Escure (2004), for example, remarks that Garifuna is an endangered language in Belize and Honduras, as it is only spoken fluently by those over fifty years of age.[8]

A possible exception might be Hopkins village, which has been claimed to still raise children to speak Garifuna natively, though this claim is not without controversy. There is, however, a clear perception of Hopkins by Garifuna people in other communities as being the last bastion of the Garifuna language in Belize. For example, the National Garifuna Council's website asserts: "However, it is only in one village—Hopkins—that young children still learn [Garifuna] as their native language" (ISCR n.d.). We heard this same statement—repeated almost as a refrain—by everyone we surveyed in Seine Bight. Further, Ravindranath (2009), who based her dissertation fieldwork in Hopkins from 2007 to 2008, reports that many children in Hopkins do indeed learn both Garifuna and Kriol as first languages.[9] She further expresses hope about the future of the Garifuna language in Hopkins. Citing social and economic factors such as changing emigration patterns and the growing tourism industry in the village, she suggests it might be possible to achieve a stable bilingualism in Hopkins and thus continued use of the Garifuna language. The idea is rooted in the belief that the tourist industry could provide local jobs for Hopkins residents, allowing them to live at home and so maintain ties with the Garifuna community rather than emigrating elsewhere for work.[10]

It has been almost a decade since Ravindranath's work in Hopkins, and to our knowledge no follow-up work has been conducted. The tourist industry is indeed growing furiously in Hopkins, as it is located near some of the most beautiful beaches in Belize. Similar to the situation we will discuss below with respect to Seine Bight, luxury development is fast encroaching on Hopkins as well, squeezing it inward from all sides. As Ravindranath (2009: 179) writes, "The purchase of large pieces of land at the edges of the village by expatriate North Americans, has created a potentially volatile situation in which the village is running out of room in which to grow." Consider this description of the Plantation, a luxury development planned for immediately north of Seine Bight. The description is taken from a 2011 study on the ecological impact of the proposed development on the peninsula: "The Plantation proposes to add an additional 10,000+ people over the next 5 years to an area that is only 16 miles long and at maximum one-half mile wide. Belizean people will become a small minority of the Peninsula population. If the development capacity of The Plantation is fully realized, this would increase the Peninsula population by about four or five times, ultimately changing the very nature of the entire area forever" (University of Belize, Natural Resources Management Program 2011: 15). This loss of physical space to foreign luxury development—as well as large land purchases by missionary religious groups in other districts—is a recurring problem for Garifuna villages as well as those of other ethnic groups elsewhere in Belize.

In what follows, we report on our recent fieldwork on Garifuna language use in Seine Bight, as well as the prospects we see for the future of the language there, and the situational circumstances we see leading to this future. As no linguistic fieldwork has been conducted in Seine Bight since Escure (2004), it is worthwhile to revisit this important Garifuna site to reconsider the state of the language.

A Case Study in Seine Bight

Seine Bight village is located approximately halfway out on the Placencia Peninsula in southern Belize. Settled by Garifuna migrants from Honduras in the mid-nineteenth century, it is located approximately ninety miles north of Punta Gorda and forty miles south of Dangriga, the two largest Garifuna communities in the country today. The most recent national census reports approximately 1,300 residents in Seine Bight, with a large majority of these being Garifuna, but also including small numbers of other ethnicities, such as Mestizo and Chinese. The large Garifuna majority in the village, as well as its long settlement history and its current proximity to rapidly growing tourist developments, make it a valuable site for a study of this kind.

Seine Bight is a long, narrow village situated on a peninsula enveloped by a lagoon to the west and the Caribbean Sea to the east (map 3). The village is approximately one mile long and perhaps a half-mile wide in places. Map 3 shows the central core of the village. To the immediate north and south of the village pictured here are rapidly growing luxury developments of mostly U.S. and European ownership. Four miles to the south is Placencia, which was a Creole fishing village until perhaps the 1990s, at which point it began to undergo massive tourist development and is now one of the most popular tourist destinations in Belize, with mostly foreign-owned tourist businesses, including a luxury resort owned by film director Francis Ford Coppola. As Carol Key (2002: 78) writes, "Before 1991 it was still possible for Belizeans to purchase property in [Placencia]; however, by 1994 the price for land had risen beyond what a Belizean could afford."[11]

Seine Bight villagers historically depended on subsistence fishing and agriculture, with Garifuna men also frequently migrating

Map 3. Seine Bight

elsewhere for work and returning home to the village. In the last several decades this migration has grown to include women and children and has become less cyclical, with migrants often emigrating permanently, usually to large urban areas in the United States such as Los Angeles and New York City. As Escure (2004: 38) writes, "There are no official figures on emigration, but it is estimated that the population living outside Central America is at least as large as that residing in the region." Today, traditional fishing and agricultural wage labor have largely given way to livelihoods associated with tourism—that is, selling goods to tourists, working in tourist-oriented businesses in Placencia, and so on—with women doing the latter more frequently. The decline in fishing is due to a number of factors. Most prominent is the shrinking numbers of fish in the surrounding waters—due to overfishing, pollution, increased population, and other factors—which makes it necessary to work longer and harder to make ends meet as a fisherman. Quite simply, it is easier to earn a living in the service industry (see Key 2002; and University of Belize, Natural Resources Management Program 2011: 33). Remittances from relatives living elsewhere also continue to be a vital contribution to the village economy (see Palacio 1982; Key 2002; and Escure 2004).

Linguistic Fieldwork in Seine Bight

There has been very little work done on attitudes and use of the Garifuna language in Seine Bight, or discussion of its declining status. The closest work we know of is Escure's 2004 article on grammatical structure in the Garifuna language.[12] Similarly, Ravindranath 2009 discusses language use in Seine Bight briefly; however, the dissertation is primarily concerned with Garifuna language in Hopkins, approximately thirty miles to the north. To get a picture of contemporary language use in Seine Bight, our 2016 fieldwork relied on formal surveys as well as ethnographic observations in a range of social settings. The results of both of these methods suggest that Garifuna language is indeed in dramatic decline in Seine Bight, and that thirteen years later the language is likely in more dire straits than was reported in Escure 2004.

In May 2016, we conducted language status surveys in Seine Bight with fifty village residents. Participants were evenly distributed across gender and divided into two approximately equally weighted age groups: one composed of people thirty-five years and under, and the other thirty-six and older. Surveys contained a total of thirty-three questions. Some of the questions were demographic and required only simple answers. Others invited lengthy discussion. We were primarily interested in finding out who was believed to speak Garifuna (that is, which age group and gender) and in what types of social situations it was likely to be spoken. We also wanted to know what sorts of attitudes residents had toward Garifuna and the other languages spoken in the surrounding area. We used several direct questions, such as (1) "What language do young people speak more?" and (2) "What language do old people speak more?" The survey also included open-ended questions, querying social situations, such as (3) "What languages are used in school/church/shops/on the street in Seine Bight?" and questions of a more personal nature, like (4) "What language do you use with your/spouse/children/grandchildren?" We also included preference questions such as, (5) "What language would you prefer be used in schools in Seine Bight? Why?" The answers to the first two questions were completely uniform. All fifty participants agreed that young people used Kriol or English, and that only much older people were capable of using Garifuna fluently. Of our fifty participants, sixteen were under twenty years of age, and only five of these sixteen reported being able to speak even a few words of Garifuna.[13] With respect to the third question, the nearly unanimous response was that Garifuna was heard in speech among the elderly or on the national Garifuna holiday, Garifuna Settlement Day, which is celebrated November 19. Regarding use of the Garifuna language in Seine Bight, the result was again essentially unanimous that the speech heard and used everywhere in the village is Kriol. Potentially the most interesting results of the survey came in responses to the fourth question. Among the participants who had spouses, children, and grandchildren, we found that those over fifty reported talking to their spouse in Garifuna, but they also reported talking to their children and grandchildren in Kriol—a couple of participants commented on their surveys that they speak to their children and grandchildren in Garifuna but that the children respond to them in Kriol. A pair of brothers in their late twenties shared a particularly touching story about their childhood, which captures the differing generational abilities in the language and the frustration and regret frequently attendant upon such situations. When the brothers were children, one of their neighbors, an elderly man, would address them in Garifuna, but they would respond to him in Kriol, as they were unable to speak the traditional language. The old man would yell and curse at the children, telling them that they were stupid and that it was their fault that their heritage was slipping away. The brothers attempted to tell this story to us in a humorous way, but it was clear from their silence that followed that it had affected them deeply.

When queried as to why the language was falling out of use, participants invariably responded that their children and grandchildren do not speak Garifuna. The results of this question offer a rather dramatic, cross-sectional depiction of the language as it diminishes across the generations. It is also telling that the villagers are explicitly aware of this intergenerational disruption of the language. We received a variety of responses to the fifth question, which were again quite telling as to the status of the language. Most participants indicated that they would prefer schools teach English over any other language, with female participants choosing English overwhelmingly. In fact, a group of teenage girls we surveyed, who were between the ages of thirteen and sixteen, burst into laughter when asked if they thought Garifuna should be taught in school, saying that there was no reason whatsoever to speak Garifuna. The most common justification given among female participants was that learning English would offer better chances of success for future job opportunities. Male participants, as young as fourteen years old, were more likely to say that Garifuna should be taught alongside English, and they frequently expressed regret that it was not.[14]

Two young women we surveyed illustrate this gender distinction especially clearly. Both under the age of eighteen, they work at a Garifuna-themed restaurant in town that specializes in Garifuna food such as *hudut*, a stew of fish, plantains, and coconut. Neither of the young women could speak Garifuna. Over the course of the interview, the girls expressed pride in being able to prepare traditional Garifuna foods, but they nonetheless indicated their preference that students learn English in school.

In sum, the surveys present a picture of the Garifuna language in Seine Bight as something of an artifact of the elderly, with little evidence of intergenerational transmission and bleak prospects for the long-term health of the language. However, quantitative surveys of the type just reported are frequently criticized for a variety of reasons. It has been argued, for example, that direct self-reporting of attitude and usage facts is not always reliable. Survey questions can be worded in such ways that participants do not understand what researchers are asking. Similarly, numerous factors surrounding the context in which surveys are taken have been shown to influence results. Most worrisome, however, is that participants' perceptions of their own attitude and usage tendencies don't always match with observed behavior.[15] We therefore followed up on the survey results with ethnographic observations in a variety of social situations. The results of our ethnographic work not only confirm but provide an even starker portrait of the state of the Garifuna language in the village.

Ethnographic Fieldwork

In addition to the fifty quantitative surveys discussed above, we followed up with ethnographic observations in a wide variety of social settings. According to the results of the first question above, it appears that older people in Seine Bight still speak mainly Garifuna and that younger people speak mainly Kriol. Our ethnographic work did not find this to be the case. Certainly the younger people spoke Kriol in all social settings in which we observed them; however, we heard very little Garifuna spoken by anyone of any age.

We observed a wide range of social settings: including those in which the nature of our presence as researchers was known, as well as those in which it was not. For example, when we were invited into people's homes to talk and spend time with their families, we played a direct role in the social situation and very likely affected the nature of the language that was used. However, we also observed many social situations in which we played no role whatsoever. These were by far the most common, and we mention a few to give the reader an idea of the naturalness of the situations and data. Everywhere we went, we listened, whether we were sitting behind people conversing at a bus stop or whether we were walking in the aisles of a grocery store, having lunch at a Garifuna restaurant, resting on the front porch of a community center during a teen function, watching a softball game as players called to each other as well as observers on the sidelines, standing in the shade on the schoolyard listening to children at play, sitting in a church pew or on the front porch before a Sunday service, observing on the street as mothers disciplined their children, or pausing as the sounds of a violent argument between two lovers spilled out of a house and into the sandy street where we stood. In all such situations, we heard only Kriol, and no Garifuna spoken by young or old. These kinds of observations—and the distance from which we made them—do much to obviate the problems of the observer's paradox. The people we listened to were not concerned with us, and we were in no way participating in their lives or interactions. We are confident that the language we heard spoken was natural for the situations, with our presence playing no influencing role.[16]

This ethnographic experience not only verifies what was found in the surveys but strengthens the claims that can be made based upon them. It is also testifies to the importance of mixed method fieldwork. Survey results suggest that older folk speak primarily Garifuna; yet this was not our experience in any of the numerous situations we observed. This leaves one to conclude that the Garifuna spoken by the older generations is limited to a small number of special or closed-door situations to which we did not have access. It also suggests that the number of situations in which even the elderly find it useful to speak Garifuna have diminished substantially. In essence, the observational work presents an even bleaker picture of the state of the language than is revealed by the surveys, as the observations seem to indicate that most people in Seine Bight do not use Garifuna at all in day-to-day situations.

Pressures on the Garifuna Language in Seine Bight

A variety of factors over the years have adversely affected the state of the Garifuna language in Seine Bight. Some of these could be considered general factors of globalization, which have arguably affected the state of the Garifuna language in most villages in the country, including Seine Bight. Some, however, are factors specific to Seine Bight. We'll begin with the first group of more general pressures, including cultural contact and erosion, which we suggest have weakened the state of the language in general.

The extensive transnational movements of the Garifuna people are well known. As mentioned above, Garifuna communities in New York City and Los Angeles are now arguably larger than those in Central America. Most Garinagu in Belize have relatives who have emigrated to the United States and are in close contact with external cultural standards as a result. The easy availability of U.S. media contributes to this contact as well, as television and smart phones, Facebook and YouTube, are ubiquitous in Garifuna households. This onslaught of exposure to influential external belief systems has undoubtedly diminished traditional aspects of Garifuna culture, which in turn undermines a crucial foundation for maintaining the language. For example, the traditional Garifuna religion, which includes ancestor veneration and possession trances, is in sharp conflict with the much larger, mainstream Abrahamic religious systems with which the Garifuna are constantly in contact.[17] Historically, the Garifuna have been able to maintain their religious system even in the face of such contact (see Cayetano 1974). It is not clear that this is still the case in Belize. Nancie González (1988: 92), for example, reports that at the time of her research, the Garifuna *dugu* ceremonies, which are central to the Garifuna religion and include ancestral spirit possession, were believed by many to have become "big business" and too expensive for most Garifuna to afford.[18] She cites a Honduran *buwiye* (holy man) who believed that the "Belizean Garifuna had lost the essential holiness of the ritual in their efforts to outdo each other in the amount of money spent." In a sense, then, although the ritual itself persists, it's not clear that it holds the same spiritual and cultural weight as in times past.

González also notes that Garifuna religious beliefs are frequently abandoned by emigrants from Central America as they adapt to the cultural settings in their new home, usually the United States. As she writes, "Many of the more widely traveled Garifuna of the past fifty years, especially those who were in more or less constant contact with American or English employers, are openly skeptical, if not contemptuous, of the whole ritual complex" (González 1998: 91). One can imagine, then, the effects of this on their countrymen who remain behind in the village and witness these emigrants returning with an improved socioeconomic status and the prestige that often accompanies it. We suggest that as these cultural underpinnings are muted or spread thin over time, the need and ability to maintain the language is further compromised.

In essence what we are describing is a reduction of situations in which the traditional language is seen to be useful.[19] As we will discuss below, speaking Garifuna does not seem to provide the people with obvious socioeconomic advantages; and, if important cultural institutions such as religious rites begin to erode as well, it is that much more difficult to see a healthy path forward for the language.[20]

In terms of socioeconomic advantages, it is not clear what the benefits of speaking Garifuna would be for the residents of Seine Bight. Employment in the surrounding tourist industry requires facility in Kriol or English. This is similarly true for nearby agricultural work, in which the Spanish language would also be welcome. However, there are no local markets, trade venues, or other areas of employment in which speaking Garifuna is a requirement, and thus no obvious platform of support for the language in this area. We can contrast this situation with, for example, those described in Mufwene 2003 with respect to the African languages Lingala, Swahili, and Hausa, in which indigenous languages are similarly in contact with major European languages, but in which the indigenous languages do not seem to be in an endangering competition. Mufwene describes two-tiered economic systems here, in which vital roles for the indigenous languages continue to exist alongside European languages. As he writes, "Despite the dominant use of European languages in the media, the indigenous African languages maintain such an important role in the socio-economic lives of most black Africans that there is no particular reason to see them in competition now with the European languages." The same cannot be said for the Garifuna language.

Closer to home, a comparison of the Garifuna situation with that of the Belizean Mennonites is similarly instructive. According to the 2010 census, the Garifuna population in Belize is almost twice as large as that of the Mennonites. However, there are more German speakers in Belize than Garifuna speakers. The circumstances of the two communities seem to predict this result. For example, the Mennonites control a large percentage of the agricultural production in Belize. They also mostly live apart from the general Belizean population, with a strong sense of community identity grounded in religion as well as their internal economic establishment. We also see much less contact with international tourism and miniscule Mennonite emigration to other countries. Lastly, the Garifuna boast a 95 percent literacy rate in English, while Mennonites report only 22 percent literacy. The Mennonites, whose Plautdietsch language seems to be relatively secure, thus contrast with the Garifuna in almost every possible way with regard to language vitality.

affects ethnic Lg usage

Returning to Seine Bight specifically, the rapidly growing tourism industry on both sides of the village and the effects this must be having on Garifuna language and culture cannot be overstated. As you drive into Seine Bight from the north side of the peninsula, you are immediately struck by the high-end real estate signage and sprawl of condominiums and foreign-owned resorts leading right up to the Seine Bight city limit sign. The same is true when one leaves Seine Bight heading south toward Placencia. There is virtually nowhere for Seine Bight to grow, enveloped as the town is between expensive foreign developments. We noted foreign real estate listings within Seine Bight as well, and we were told that this was the first time in recent history that property was listed this way in the town. The effect of approaching Seine Bight and driving through it from north to south is passing from a wealthy tourist destination through a mile of abject poverty and then back to the wealthy tourist destination. It seems only a matter of time before Seine Bight itself will be sold out from underneath its residents.

With such close proximity to the tourist businesses, one might hold out hope that Seine Bight residents will find employment and thus a path toward economic, cultural, and linguistic security. This does not seem to be happening, however. Writing in 2002, Key reported that Seine Bight residents did supply labor to the tourist businesses. In our observations fourteen years later, there seem to be far more Spanish/Mestizo employees in the resorts surrounding Seine Bight. And discussion with multiple tourist business owners revealed attitudes toward both Creoles and Garifuna as "not hard working," and that "unfortunately" it was better to hire Spanish-speaking immigrants from Guatemala and Honduras or Mestizo Belizeans from Cayo District. Our ethnographic observations in the larger more prestigious resorts on the peninsula confirmed that this was indeed the case, with the exception of the occasional Garifuna woman working in Placencia.

It seems that in Seine Bight, then, both economic and cultural forces have conspired to squeeze out the Garifuna language, and that barring some large and far-reaching change, the language will be very soon lost there.

Forces of Change

As in other dynamic linguistic contexts, the factors driving language change, language shift, and endangerment on the Central American Caribbean coast have largely been unexplored. As an organizing principle in this book, the concept of "language ecology," has allowed us to consider the relationships and place of a language in its larger social and cultural contexts. According to Haugen (1972: 325), one of the earliest thinkers on the subject,

> Language ecology may be defined as the study of interactions between any given language and its environment. . . . The true environment of a language is the society that uses it as one of its codes. Language exists only in the minds of its users, and it only functions in relating these users to one another and to nature, i.e. their social and natural environment. Part of its ecology is therefore psychological: its interaction with other languages in the minds of bi- and multilingual speakers. Another part of its ecology is sociological: its interaction with the society in which it functions as a medium of communication.[1]

The emerging body of work on language-contact issues in the Central American Caribbean coastal region focuses on contact-induced change in the phonologies and morphosyntactic systems of area minority languages. This scholarship has shed light on the intensity of the contact in question, but it has focused on attitudes of the speakers in the contact situations.[2] While attitudes and intensity are certainly constituents of the linguistic ecologies of the languages we have examined, our attention to social factors conditioning language attitudes in coastal Belize has highlighted factors that have not been thoroughly explored in the fields of linguistics and Latin American studies, and certainly not in an interdisciplinary fashion.

Anne Sutherland (1998) highlights Belize's abrupt transition from colony to postmodern nation "influenced by strong transnational movements and ideas such as environmentalism, liberalization of the economy, democracy, international tourism, and the international drug trade" (3). The young nation remains one of the most ethnically diverse in Central America, and the country's transition into independence ushered changes in the ways that the new citizens identified themselves and their compatriots. Le Page and Tabouret-Keller (1985) reported on the changing conceptions of identity between ethnic Creole, Mayan, and Garifuna groups, as well as the multilingual identities of these same minority groups in the Cayo District at the dawn of independence. Decades later, our 2012–16 fieldwork on Kriol, Mopan, and Garifuna in coastal Belize has allowed us to identify several factors that constitute the ecologies of minority languages in an empirically different context. In the discussion below, we examine the most significant aspects of these ecologies and their contribution to the state of transitional bilingualism (and likely language loss) in which these languages currently reside.

1. **Integration into the National Fold.** Belize gained its independence from Great Britain in 1981. The Belizean Constitution was signed in September 1981 and went into effect immediately. This document provides criteria for determining citizenship and specifies the rights, protections, and responsibilities of its citizens and, notably, contains an explicit protection against slavery and discrimination on the basis of sex, race, place of origin, political opinions, color, or creed. The important acknowledgement of (1) marginalization arising from a rural/urban and coastal/inland "place of origin," as well as (2) "color" as a result of the legacy of a pigmentocratic system that has been in place since the era of slavery are important aspects of this constitution.

2. **Cultural Prominence of Creoles.** Historically, Belize ex-

perienced an atypical institution of slavery, which saw small groups of slaves in mobile logging camps, often working alongside whites, rather than the large sugar plantations found elsewhere in the Caribbean. As such, the social position of slaves and their descendants in Belize, which included many Creoles, was less regimented than other Caribbean slave experiences. Some of the Creoles ultimately enjoyed a better relationship with colonial whites, and this has had lasting ramifications in terms of cultural prominence. For example, most high-ranking elected officials—including former and current prime ministers—continue to be Creoles today, even though ethnic Creoles are a minority in the country. It is well known that when a group is prominent or prestigious, their language will typically share in this high regard. Finally, since independence in 1981, it has been the Creole identity to which the country has turned to distinguish itself from that of British colonialism; again, this is in spite of the fact that ethnic Creoles are not a majority in the country.

3. **Citizenship and Foreignness.** The Belizean Constitution signed in 1981 provided for an "economic citizenship" provision that granted citizenship to individuals who made "a substantial contribution to the economy and/or well-being of Belize." While Belize was the destination of Honduran, Salvadoran, and Guatemalan immigrants fleeing civil wars in their countries of origin, it also became the destination for a large number of retirees from the United States and Canada who settled in Belize. The provision was repealed in 2001 following widespread criticism, and tension between groups over "rightful citizenship" in Belize is permeable to this day. The tensions are felt in rural areas, where the Belizean government is said to have granted plots of land to Spanish-speaking Central Americans, as well as seaside urban areas where landownership is dramatically concentrated in the hands of Anglophone U.S.-Belizean and Canadian-Belizean dual citizens. Meanwhile, ongoing bor-

der disputes with Guatemala contribute to a growing sense of Belizean nationalism, which is symbolized in Creole culture and language.

4. **Tourism and Private Property.** Villas, cattle ranches, seafront lots, golf courses, private islands, and private cays are available for purchase to foreigners (with or without Belizean citizenship) with little to no restrictions, promoting large-scale construction of condos, beach homes, resorts, and retail centers to attract tourists. At the time of this writing, Sotheby's—with headquarters on Barrier Reef Drive, San Pedro Town, Belize—lists properties for US$9.9 million, and even a much more "modest" website advertises a 5,000-acre property boasting "a spectacular display of wildlife, with thousands of Mahogany and Royal Palm trees" in Ladyville, home to the Belize City Airport, for $10 million. Meanwhile, U.S. actor Leonardo DiCaprio and an associate purchased Blackadore Caye, a 104-acre private island off the coast of Belize, for $1.75 million, with the intention of developing it into an ecoresort, with houses built on the island expected to sell for $5–15 million. To put those prices into perspective, the Central Intelligence Agency listed Belize's GDP per capita at $8,600 in 2015 and stated that 41 percent of the population fell below the poverty line. As census data and observers have noted, owning a home, particularly in the coastal Belizean districts, is beyond reach for many Belizean nationals.

5. **Decline of Traditional Livelihoods (Fishing and Hunting).** As in other countries where tourism contributes greatly to the nation's GDP, environmental decisions in Belize are made to serve the expanding ecotourism industry. This has had an impact on local fishing industries, in addition to the competition between small-scale fishermen and a large-scale industry in the same ocean waters. Poaching is also common, leading to depletion of the commonly sought species. Further, and perhaps most alarming, is the designation of an increasing number of rural areas as national parks, nature reserves, and wildlife sanctuaries. While na-

ture parks and sanctuaries are appealing to foreign tourists, this kind of action has led historically to displacement of indigenous Mayan and Garifuna communities and has had a direct impact on food security as hunting and fishing become restricted at best, and prohibited at worst.

6. **Educational Institutions.** The Belizean Constitution guaranteed free public education for its citizens, and made schooling compulsory for children aged six to fourteen. Ten years after independence, the Belizean government expressed in a World Bank report its plan to promote economic growth by "providing its citizens with a sound foundation of basic education on which effective future employee training programs can build" (cited in Murnane, Mullens, and Willet 1996: 146). Though it was originally modeled after the British system, U.S. educational systems and Jesuit missionaries have had a strong effect on private and public Belizean education. For example, it is commonly believed that St. Catherine Academy and St. John's College High School (which held its 2014 prom at the prestigious Radisson Fort George in Belize City) are the best high schools in the country. These educational institutions reinforce overt and covert language attitudes toward English and Kriol, since teachers are not only pillars of society—especially in rural contexts—but also are responsible for the educational baseline of Belizean citizens.

7. **Religious Institutions.** Bolland (1988: 210) writes that along with race and language, religion "defines and overlaps 'ethnic groups'" in Belize. Protestant British colonialism had a lasting impact on the Creole community, whose enslaved and emancipated ancestors practiced the Anglican, Methodist, and Baptist traditions. Catholicism first arrived on the shores of British Honduras as it did elsewhere in the Americas—as a weapon of colonialism. Mayan struggles against Spanish settlement on their lands in British Honduras halted a long-term establishment of Spanish friars and Catholic churches. By the time British Honduras became independent Belize, however, 60 percent of the popu-

lation identified as Catholic.[3] Since then, the number of Belizeans affiliated with all of these religions has dropped significantly. Results from the most recent census indicate that 40 percent of Belizeans identify as Catholic, 18.3 percent practice fundamentalist and evangelical religions, and 15.5 percent indicate they are not religious, leaving much smaller percentages of Belizeans who practice other ancestral or Protestant religions. The spectrum of beliefs from agnostic to evangelical is broadest among the Creole community, Mayas are likely to be practicing Catholics or evangelical Christians, and Garifuna communities are the least involved in the growing evangelical missions in the country.

8. **Generational Differences in Religion, Education, Social Relationships.** Whereas religion was central in the lives of their grandparents and parents, for most teenagers in contemporary Belize (with the exception of those who practice Pentecostal religions) religion is just one among many factors influencing their decision making. For these youth, "educational markers are eclipsing religious and subcultural rituals regarding movement from childhood to adulthood" (Anderson-Fye 2007: 77). Although grandparents and parents believe that young people are more independent than they were, this is not perceived as a negative attribute; instead, it is generally correlated with educational attainment. Family networks continue to be important to Belizeans across generations, even as transnational emigration and migration over the last thirty-five years have had an impact on how often family members see each other. Furthermore, young people's friendships are no longer limited to their cousin-kin but extended to include Belizean peers met in high school—from different ethnic and class backgrounds— and even foreigners met through online chat rooms and social networks.[4] Perhaps one of the most important features of the young people in Belize is that "personal identity is tied to national identity for most Belizean adolescents. Great pride is taken in being Belizean" (Anderson-Fye 2007: 79).

9. **Gender Dynamics.** Educational opportunities have signifi-

cantly affected gender dynamics, since they provide young Belizean women with alternatives to early marriage and young childbearing. Mass media has likewise had a major influence on teenagers and their mothers, since talk shows and reality television have given women vocabulary and emotional patterning (Anderson-Fye 2003). Certain behaviors, such as spousal maltreatment or male infidelity might have been normative in the romantic relationships of grandparents, but expectations of partners have changed for parents and teenagers today. Similarly, preferential treatment of boys over girls in many aspects of life, from schooling to household tasks, has changed as foreign media and the changing composition of the Belizean workforce alters former conceptions about men and women. Belizeans are aware of global discussions about gender equity, and this is certainly a driving force, but the most salient force at work here is economic, as it becomes evident that the service industry requires female workers and that those workers must have a high school education at the very least. Creole and Garifuna families have historically had female heads of household, while Spanish and Mayan families have traditionally had male heads of household, but across ethnic groups, most young people have expectations of personal economic success and gender equity in relationships (Anderson-Fye 2003). Belizean women take great pride in their femininity, and curvaceous bodies are valued as Wilk's (1993) study of Belizean beauty pageants demonstrates, yet so too are women's industriousness and intelligence.

10. **Bi- and multilingualism.** Belize is a highly bi- and multilingual country, with most of its citizens able to speak two or more languages. The Kriol language is the mother tongue of ethnic Creoles, but it also serves as a lingua franca for the rest of the country. Thus, regardless of their native language—whether it be Spanish, Mopan, Kekchi, Garifuna, or other tongues—most Belizeans can speak Kriol. In the last few decades, however, since independence and given the factors listed in this section, the Kriol language has taken on

the social meaning of "authentic" Belizean identity. Furthermore, the number of informal and formal contexts in which it is used has grown significantly in the last thirty-five years. This social elevation and ubiquity of Kriol has consequences for the other minority languages in the country. As discussed above, bi- and multilingualism can lead to permanent language shift under certain circumstances. This current state of affairs, which could be called a "transitional bilingualism," is one of the most significant factors leading to an increase in the number of speakers. Concurrently, we observe a rapid decline in speakers' use of other Belizean minority languages.

It is not lost upon us as we reach the end of our study that several of these factors overlap. Nor do we claim that this is an exhaustive list of all the factors that constitute the ecology of the languages, especially the minority languages, of Belize. We do hope, however, that the sketches we have provided of these factors—bi- and multilingualism, shifting gender dynamics, widened generation gaps, changes in religious and educational institutions, the rise of tourism, the decline of local fishing industries, the cultural prominence of Creoles, and the "integration" of hitherto isolated geographic areas—present a more systematic picture of language shift and language endangerment. The complexity of these processes cannot be understated, especially in lush contexts where growing and emerging tourist economies are persistently driving change in geographic and linguistic landscapes.

As we have suggested in our study of minority languages in Belize and in our discussion of minority languages across the Americas, the socioeconomic and political contexts of tropical tongues are subject to a plethora of variants, making it difficult to develop and test hypotheses about the development of the languages. To complicate matters further, no two minority languages are on equal footing, even when they are spoken in the same geographically bound site. Linguistic hierarchies come into play during key historical turning periods when national and regional identities are called into question. And yet, as we have seen, the linguistic vitality of any tropical tongue at the very minimum depends on the stability of four pillars in its environment: language policy and the mechanisms for its implementation, passionate proponents of the language at the forefront of a grassroots language movement, ideologies about the linguistic dimension of national identity, and positive language attitudes rooted in the belief that the language is vital to those whose lives and livelihoods are at stake.

Herodotus advised his readers to read geography historically and to read all history geographically. In a similar vein, we have suggested that geography be read linguistically and that linguistics be read geographically in order to examine the complex ecologies of tropical languages. Geographically situated between the Tropic of Cancer and the Tropic of Capricorn, the (linguistic) climate of "the tropics" has never been temperate.[5] Subject to a variety of negative attitudes and policies aimed at taming their growth, so to speak, the indigenous and creole languages of the tropical Central American Caribbean coast have been razed for centuries, from the colonial period through the postindependence period, in order to till the soil for the English, Spanish, French, Dutch, and Portuguese. In spite of this, many of the lush tongues of this coastal strip thrived until recently. They have been spoken on linguistic islands, in jungles, at the foothills of "mountains" concealing ancient pyramids,[6] on rimlands where European ships couldn't dock, in swampy areas, and in settlements around lagoons. Just like the mangroves of these very same tropics, they have lived a rich life "on the edge," enabling those who depend on them to become brilliant adaptors to changing tides. And, in a manner even more analogous to those very same mangroves, the vitality of tropical tongues is threatened by encroaching tourism, as the sites in which they have hitherto flourished become depopulated or leveled in order to facilitate the construction of the housing developments, roads, port facilities, hotels, golf courses, and ecoresorts that are the hallmark of the bourgeoning service and tourist economy of Belize.

Notes

1. Nicholas Spykman (1944) first used the term *rimland* to describe the maritime fringe of a country or continent, contrasting it with *heartland*, with its geopolitical focus on the interior of a nation or continent. Literary critic Ian Smart (1984) used the concept of rimlands to develop a theory of black Central American literature.

2. For a fascinating discussion of language ecologies in Brazil, see Mufwene 2014.

3. The language status of Miskito as measured by *Ethnologue*'s EGIDS is 2, which indicates that the language is used in education, work, mass media, and government within major administrative subdivisions of Nicaragua. It is spoken as a mother tongue mainly by adults, who also use English, Nicaraguan Creole English, and Spanish, and it is spoken as an L2 by speakers of Mayangna and Spanish-speaking Mestizos. In addition, there are published materials, including a dictionary, grammar, and Bible in the language. *Ethnologue* 2017c.

4. The language status of Nicaragua Creole English as measured by *Ethnologue*'s EGIDS is 3, indicating that the language is used in work and mass media and, like Miskito, it is used and sustained by institutions beyond the home and community. Speakers of the language also use English and Spanish, and the linguistic community has grown to include Garifuna, Miskito, Rama, and Spanish-speaking Mestizos who use it as an L2. *Ethnologue* 2017d.

5. For detailed analysis of annexation and its repercussions, see Hale 1994. For an account of the six coastal communities (Mestizo, Criollo, Miskito, Garifuna, Rama, and Sumo) in Nicaragua, as well as details about the development of creole languages on the Nicaraguan shore, see Holm 1983; and López Alonzo 2016.

6. The precedent for this language was Decree 571 promoted by an organization called MISURASATA (Miskitus, Sumus, Ramas, and Sandinistas United Together) and passed by the Sandinista government in 1980. The decree stated that "the maternal language constitutes a fundamental factor in the existence of persons and peoples and is a determining factor in the process of integration and consolidation of National Unity." Article 1 authorized "instruction at the pre-primary and in the first four grades of primary in Miskitu and English languages in the schools in the zone" where the respective indigenous and Creole communities resided (Arnove and Ovando 1993).

7. Extraordinary work on language contact in Mexico and Paraguay is developed by Carol Klee and Andrew Lynch. We direct the reader to their *El español en contacto con otras lenguas* (2009) for a more comprehensive history of Nahuatl and Guaraní and their lexical, syntactic, phonological, semantic, and pragmatic impact on the Mexican and Paraguayan varieties of Spanish.

8. There was a paucity of Spaniards living in New Spain and this monolingual Castilian-speaking community seldom ventured out of the capital, resulting in the virtual absence of interaction with monolingual and bilingual indigenous populations (Hidalgo 2001: 59).

9. The language status of Kaqchikel as measured by *Ethnologue*'s EGIDS is 4 (Educational), indicating that it is a recognized language, that nearly all parents pass Kaqchikel to their children, and that it is used among all age groups. In addition, it is used as an L2 by speakers of K'iché. It is in vigorous use, with standardization and literature being sustained through a widespread system of institutionally supported primary and secondary schools. It is also used in radio programs and online in a variety of social media platforms.

10. Barbara Cifuentes and José Luis Moctezuma (2006: 204), for example, describe a steady increase in the number of people who identify as bilingual in Mexico, from 37.7 percent of the population to 81.4 percent of the population in 2000.

11. According to *Ethnologue*, the languages spoken in Chiapas are, by category, Chiapanec (9 Dormant), Chicomuceltec (9 Dormant), Chol (5 Developing), Chuj (6b Threatened), Jakalteco (8a Moribund), Kanjobal (6a Vigorous), Lacandon (5 Developing), Mam (5 Dispersed), Mocho (8a Moribund), Tectitec (7 Shifting), Tojolabal (5 Developing), Tzetzal (5 Developing), Tzotzil (6b Threatened), and Zoque (6a Vigorous).

12. An excellent resource with a full description of the official, governmentally decreed language policy in Argentina, Bolivia, Brazil, Colombia, Ecuador, Guatemala, Mexico, Nicaragua, Paraguay, Peru, and Venezuela since the 1990s can be found in García, López, and Makar 2010.

13. See note 7 above.

14. Despite decades of research, many unresolved questions remain as to the roles of internal or external motivations in language change. As Sarah Thomason (2010: 33) writes, "In spite of dramatic progress toward explaining linguistic changes made in recent decades by historical linguists, variationists, and experimental linguists, it remains true that we have no adequate explanation for the vast majority of all linguistic changes that have been discovered. Worse, it may reasonably be said that we have no full explanation for any linguistic change, or for the emergence and spread of any linguistic variant. The reason is that, although it is often easy to find a motivation for

an innovation, *the combinations of social and linguistic* factors that favor the success of one innovation and the failure of another are so complex that we can never (in my opinion) hope to achieve deterministic predictions in this area" (emphasis ours).

15. From the late nineteenth century through the first half of the twentieth, internally motivated change was considered the rule by most historical linguists. Beginning in the early 1950s, however, the importance of contact and resulting social implications have begun to be recognized as playing a, if not the, major role in language change. See Thomason 2006 for more detailed discussion of this shift in thought over the decades.

16. Even beyond creoles, however, clear examples of contact affecting the structure of the recipient language can be found. For example, if numerous lexical items are borrowed from one language to another, there can be systematic repercussions for the phonology or morphosyntax of the recipient language. See, for example, discussion in Sankoff 2004; Thomason 2006; and the many sources therein.

17. The Toledo Maya Council—as well as many of our participants—uses both *the Maya* and *the Mayas* to refer to members of the community. For instance, the Council's resolution states: "The Maya will have rights to develop and own this land," and that "the Maya have the right to promote their culture" (1998). Although *Mayans* would be more prevalent in the field of Latin American studies, our goal in this book is to be faithful to the terms most commonly used by the communities we surveyed. In the same vein, we capitalize the term *Mestizo* as it most often appears in Belize (although it is written in lowercase in many other Latin American contexts), and we spell the language spoken by the majority of indigenous people in Belize *Kekchi* (as opposed to Q'eqchi') since our participants have done so in our surveys.

CHAPTER ONE

1. The arrival of thousands of immigrants to Belize throughout the twentieth century may have contributed to the vitality of Spanish in some areas of the country, though more research is needed in this area. It is particularly important to examine Spanish in the context of the uneven development the country has experienced, since the economic growth experienced in Belize has been concentrated on the coast instead of the interior.

2. As Hildo do Couto (2014: 76) explains, the term *language island* was coined in 1847 and incorporated into the German linguistics tradition by about 1900; the term *enclave* commonly used by Anglophone and Romance linguists is actually a translation of the German word *Sprachinsel* (language island).

3. Our fieldwork suggests that Mennonite/Plautdietsch and Chinese may constitute the last intact language islands in Belize. At the moment, there is no research to confirm this possibility.

4. The majority/minority language relationship is the bedrock of much of the work on languages in contact in Latin America. In response to the threat that European languages pose to minority languages, an even more extensive body of work has emerged in Latin America focusing on language revitalization, language preservation, and minority language pedagogy. For the most recent work in this area, see Albarracín 2016; Granadillo 2016; Haboud 2016; Julca Guerrero 2016; Rosales Caro 2016; Cardona Fuentes 2016; Hernández Cervantes 2016; Morales-Good 2016; Muyolema 2016; and Vedovato 2016.

5. The question of Belizean Spanish is complex, given the historical nature of language contact and the cyclical migration of Spanish immigrants to the country. It is beyond the scope of our project to explore Corozal, Orange Walk, and Cayo at the present time.

6. William Labov (1972: 209) defines the "observer's paradox" as follows: "The aim of linguistic research in the community must be to find out how people talk when they are not being systematically observed; yet we can only obtain this data by systematic observation." See further discussion on this topic in chapter 4.

7. Our translation: "linguistic communities in circumscribed spaces, with languages or linguistic varieties relatively clearly distinguishable from the language that surrounds them, and in which there is an awareness of their own otherness, based on a dense web of communication . . . , and which is insular rather than outwardly focused."

8. Verbal-guise tests use different speakers for each language variety tested. The goal is to conceal the identities and locational information of the speakers from the participants. See Kristiansen 2011 and the many sources therein for discussion of the history, philosophy, advantages, and disadvantages of verbal guise tests in gathering attitude data.

9. In fact, many of our informants in Belize assumed we were missionaries ourselves until they learned otherwise.

10. One of the participants commented that he and his wife had known the anthropologist Eve Danziger, who had visited the community in the late 1990s, and that they had taught her Mopan on her trips to the village.

11. See Ferguson 1959, which is the classic treatment of "diglossia," and the wealth of literature that has been written on the subject since that time. "Topics" here can be considered akin to the speech genres of Mikhail Bakhtin (1950: 60), which "reflect the specific conditions and goals of each such area not only through their content (thematic) and linguistic style, that is, the

selection of the lexical, phraseological, and grammatical resources of the language, but above all through their compositional structure."

12. See, for example, Fishman 2004; Dorian 2004; and the many sources therein.

CHAPTER TWO

1. See Escure 1997: 28–39; Decker 2005; and Salmon 2015 for a sociohistorical outline of Belizean Kriol, and suggestions as to the putative origins of Kriol in contact between Africans, Europeans, and Miskito Indians in the eighteenth and nineteenth centuries.

2. Similarly, Governor General (and linguist) Sir Colville Young (2002: 12) wrote of the relative stigma of Kriol among Belizeans almost fifteen years ago: "While this stigma is slowly being lessened by work such as that being carried out by the Belize Kriol Project and by some attention being placed on Kriol's possible judicious use in the classrooms, it will take a long time to root it out—if it is ever rooted out—and in the process there may well emerge fierce language conflicts, rivalries, and divisiveness, all of which a young nation like Belize hardly needs."

3. Yet, as Ken Decker (2005) notes, this number is likely too high, as many Kriol words sound like English words but have different meanings and grammar. For example, Geneviève Escure (2008: 578) notes that "morphemes from the lexifier language, such as 'yet,' 'also,' 'even,' or 'still,' (and others) are found . . . in functions that have no exact equivalents in their respective superstrates."

4. This idea of "close but not close enough, thus deficient" is exceedingly common in creole environments in which creole languages are taken to be broken versions of their lexifiers. See, for example, discussion in Mufwene 2003.

5. See Garrett 2010: chap. 4 for discussion of the history and applicability of the verbal guise test.

6. See Rickford 1985, 1991; and Winford 1991 for discussion of the standard view of language attitudes in creole continua, with respect to creoles as lower status and acrolects or standards as higher status. As Donald Winford writes, "A general pattern of correlation between creole and the lower status on the one hand, and acrolect (English) and higher status on the other, is a fairly common feature of all the communities reported on in the literature" (572).

7. A popular saying in Belize is that Kriol is the glue that holds the country together. In a similar way, Anansi stories are a cultural touchstone in Belizean culture. Known also as *Annacy, Ananse, Nansi,* or *Nancy* stories in most Anglophone Caribbean contexts, the central character of these fables is often

a trickster spider who outsmarts tigers, elephants, lions, and other animals who reign in the forest. Scholars have traced the origin of these stories to West Africa, specifically to the Ashanti and Akan peoples of Ghana and Ivory Coast (Mosby 2003). Anansi stories survived the Middle Passage. They served as entertainment, but they also taught slaves and their descendants to outsmart their masters on the plantations. Thus the triumph of wit over physical limitations became the cornerstone of oral Caribbean culture throughout the West Indies. Preliminary work revealed that these stories are well known and well received in Belize. They are also found in Barbados, Curaçao, Haiti, Jamaica, Surinam, Trinidad and Tobago, and the Virgin Islands, as well as in Central America in Belize and Costa Rica. See Duncan 1991; Edwards 2002; Davis 2004; Ramclan and Smith 2004; and Vargas 2006.

8. As Reinhild Vandekerckhove (2010: 317) observes, "The adoption of characteristics of urban speech often appears to be part of a (conscious or subconscious) strategy of people living in small towns or in the countryside aimed at acquiring a share in the prestige associated with urbanity and the urban life style."

9. More research is needed across the Americas with regard to ethnoracial and gendered stratification in hiring practices at hotels and restaurants that cater to tourists. See Castellanos 2010 for a discussion of such practices in the growing tourist industry of the Yucatán Peninsula.

10. One wonders to what extent this pattern of culture, gender, and economics generalizes across cultures. That is, in many places around the world we see economies that traditionally depended on male labor now shifting to tourist or other modern economies in which women play a greater role and thereby accrue greater economic and personal power. In these shifting economies, then, do the displaced men consistently hold the traditional language in higher prestige?

11. Table 1 reports not on the ratings of the individual attributes, but instead on two summative groups composed of subsets of these attributes. We refer to these two groupings as *status* and *solidarity*. Our *status* grouping is composed of the attributes *attractive, educated, eloquent, intelligent,* and *modern*, while *solidarity* is composed of *friendly, hard-working, sense of humor, polite,* and *trustworthy*. The table presents means (M) of the ratings for each group pairing, and we rely on one-way analyses of variance (ANOVAs) to test for significant differences between each pairing.

12. There has also been a mixed reception to translation of *The New Testament* into Kriol. While many Belizeans are very happy with *Di Nyoo Testiment*, others have remarked to us that is sacrilegious to translate the word of God into a "broken" language.

13. *Di Nyoo Testiment* is available at www.scriptureearth.org/data/bzj

/PDF/oo-WNTbzj-web.pdf. See Salmon 2016 for further linguistic discussion of the translation.

14. See, for example, titles in the *Belizean Writers Series* published by Cubola Productions in Belize. This series was initiated in 1995, and it continues to publish an "extensive collection of . . . short stories, poems, plays, folktales and legends." The BWS catalog can be seen in its entirety at http://www.cubola.com.

CHAPTER THREE

1. The Spanish first documented their contact with Mayan communities in 1508 after a fleet sailed down the coast of what we know today as Belize. Belizean anti-Spanish warfare began with the conquest of Chetumal in 1531 and became a regionally coordinated campaign as Mayas in the area fought the Pacheco expedition of 1544 and subsequent Spanish incursions into the Belizean frontier. See Jones 1989; Oland 2009; and the many sources therein.

2. James Gregory (1972) recorded oral accounts of the resettlement and found that there were over 100 initial settlers. They settled first near Pueblo Viejo but had to move further east until they founded the village of San Antonio in order to escape Guatemalan authorities.

3. The Academia de Lenguas Mayas oversees the implementation of the 2003 Law of Mayan Languages and is thus charged with identifying Mayan languages in danger of extinction. Not all Mayan languages in Guatemala are equally endangered: Mopan and Itzá are severely endangered and are targeted for grassroots revitalization efforts, while Mam, Kiché, Kaqchikel, and Q'eqchi' are growing.

4. Yuki Tanaka (2012: 4) further observes that "all existing Mopan dictionaries (ALMG 2001, 2003, 2004), except Hofling (2011), are written in Spanish [. . . , and thus] are not accessible to most English-Mopan speakers in Belize."

5. Other important socioeconomic indicators between the two regions included the following: 93 percent of the inhabitants in Belize District had electricity from a public source compared to 56 percent in Toledo. The proportion of households using a flush toilet was highest in Belize District (92 percent) and lowest in Toledo (28 percent), and the proportion of households using a pit latrine was lowest in Belize District (5 percent) and highest in Toledo (57 percent). Lastly, 84 percent of the homes in Belize District had a fixed bath or shower in the home, compared to 23 percent of the homes in Toledo.

6. The goals of such initiatives in recent decades have been to preserve and revitalize cultural traditions while ensuring that the Mayan villages bene-

fit from tourist initiatives instead of turning profit over to foreign or central government interests. See Steinberg 1994.

7. "East Indian" is not a language. We interpret our participants' decision to state this on the survey as pride in being descendants of the cultural groups *both* of their parents represent.

8. Ravindranath (2009: 126) states in her study on Garifuna, an Afro-indigenous language spoken in Belize, that "instead of taking interviewees' responses to be indicative of their language dominance, which is difficult for anyone to judge even of themselves, I consider their response to this question to be indicative of their language attitudes."

9. For a discussion of experimental context effects on language attitude test results in general, see Garrett 2010. For a discussion of experimental context effects on attitudes in coastal Belize, see Salmon and Gómez Menjívar 2017.

10. For example, one participant in her early twenties told us that Mopan young people speak predominately Kriol: "Children don't speak Mopan. They speak Kriol and then learn English in school. If you go to the villages, you will hear Kriol."

11. Table 2 has been developed following Decker (2005: 9–10), which quotes Young 1973; and Escure 1981.

12. While the Chinese presence in Belize has not been as well documented as that of other ethnic groups in the country, Belizeans make a distinction between two major waves of Chinese immigration (in the nineteenth and twenty-first centuries). For more on the subject, see Sutherland 1998; and Robinson 2009.

13. This seems to suggest that there might be parallels between the postcolonial Belizean national project and the postdictatorship nation-building projects carried out by Sandinistas (referred to in the introduction), both of which occurred during the same period. More research in this area is needed in order to determine the degrees of influence between the two multiculturalist campaigns.

14. Longitudinal research is needed in order to determine if the youngest generation will transmit Kekchi to their children and grandchildren.

15. Belizean education policy in the *Handbook of Policies and Procedures for School Services* reads that "first languages are important vehicles for [children's] transition from home to school." Quoted in Balam and Prada Pérez 2017: 19.

16. In addition to the encroachment of national parks, nature reserves, and wildlife sanctuaries on the traditional Mopan lands, there is also a palpable fear that village territories will be sold to foreign investors, especially as construction continues on the Southern Highway to connect Toledo Dis-

trict to eastern Guatemala and the Pan-American Highway with a new border crossing. The highway runs through several Mayan villages, including San Antonio. The following is from a 2015 press release by the Belize embassy of the Republic of China:

> The development of a continuous paved highway from the northern border with Mexico to the southern border with Guatemala will boost trade, business and tourism between Belize and its neighbors as well as linking Belize to the Pan-American Highway. The construction of the section of feeder road from Mile 14 (Southern Highway), which is near Dump Village in Toledo, to Guatemala border [sic] will provide the final link in this strategic route. See details at http://www.roc-taiwan.org/bz_en/post/823.html.

17. In fact, it seems that much of the produce sold by Mayan women in the weekly markets is no longer grown in the villages but rather imported from neighboring Guatemala, a fact that very likely contributes to socioeconomic change at the local level, which in turn is a factor in the ongoing erosion of the Mopan language.

18. The *Maya Atlas*, written by the Toledo Maya Cultural Council in 1997, addressed the challenges faced by Mayan youth. In its recommendations, the council advocated for a high school in San Antonio or San Pedro Columbia that would teach languages (English, Mopan, and Kekchi), mathematics, vocational and technical courses, and arts and crafts. They also recommended land availability for young people, as well as the establishment of long-term income-producing activities beyond agriculture in indigenous communities (1997: 132), Such projects, we observe, would make remaining in Mayan communities desirable and would create more contexts in which Mayan languages could be spoken. They would also support indigenous communities as they fight to preserve their culture and assert their rights over their ancestral lands. For further reading on landmark Mayan land rights cases, see also Shoman 2011; and Murray 2012. See also the website of the Julian Cho Society: http://www.jcsbelize.org/pages/home.php.

CHAPTER FOUR

1. Garifuna is part of the Arawak language family, a South American linguistic grouping consisting of approximately forty living languages. See Aikhenvald 1999; and Ravindranath 2009.

2. For in-depth critical discussion of the various histories and hypotheses of the time leading up to 1800, see Taylor 1951; and especially González 1988. See also Shoman 2011: chap. 4; Escure 2004; and the essays in Palacio 2005.

3. The group has similarly been referred to as Charaibes Noirs, Karaib Negroes, Garif, Morenos, and other names. For discussion of this nomenclature, see Escure 2004: 38, as well as the numerous historical texts cited therein, including Breton 1665; Young 1795; and Taylor 1951.

4. The British had a variety of reasons for desiring the removal of the Black Caribs. First and foremost, they wanted the fertile land of St. Vincent for their own planting needs as well as control of the island for strategic purposes. They were also suspicious of the Black Caribs' relationship with the French and feared the Caribs might stir a rebellion among the non-Carib British slaves also residing on the island. This was especially worrisome to the British given the recent French Revolution and the slave rebellion that had been in process in Haiti since 1791. For further discussion, see González 1988: 20.

5. There are also Garifuna communities in Honduras, primarily along the coast. It is not clear what the population numbers are, however. Honduran government estimates range between 10,000 and 40,000, while cultural activists suggest numbers as high as 200,000. There are political reasons for this difference in estimates (for discussion, see Gómez Menjívar 2011); however, the problem of population counting in Honduras is compounded by the large and frequent transnational movement to Belize, the United States, and elsewhere. Similarly, Garifuna numbers in the United States are unknown due to frequent transnational movement involving both documented and undocumented immigration. The United States is believed to have the second-largest population outside of Central America, with estimates ranging from 200,000 to 300,000.

6. For detailed discussion of the linguistic diversity and environment of Punta Gorda, see Salmon and Gómez Menjívar 2016. Note that the term *Mestizo* is used to refer to the descendants of indigenous Maya and Spanish settlers in Belize. They are frequently referred to as simply "Spanish" by Belizeans. For further discussion, see the website of Belize's National Institute of Culture and History: http://www.nichbelize.org/iscr-institute-for-social-cultural-research/mestizo.html.

7. The National Garifuna Council's web page (http://ngcbelize.org) provides an informative discussion of the culture, history, and current concerns of the Garifuna people.

8. Escure's quinquagenarians would be in their sixties at the time of the present writing.

9. Others, such as Garifuna linguist E. Roy Cayetano, disagree, however. Cayetano, cited as personal communication in Ravindranath 2009: 25, suggests that the Garifuna language in Hopkins is already endangered, and that what remains of it is mostly what the villagers are trying to sell to potential tourists. Along those lines, an advertisement for a Garifuna drum school in

a May 2016 edition of the local newspaper, the *Placencia Breeze*, sits adjacent to real estate advertisements of homes in Placencia costing as much as US$1 million, and it invites tourists to "add some Garifuna flavor to your Maya temple or cacao trip!"

10. For a similar discussion of potential benefits of tourism in a Garifuna village, see Sutton 1997.

11. For a detailed history of the development of the tourism industry in Placencia, see Key 2002. See also discussion of tourism in chapter 2, above.

12. This 2004 article is based on Escure's earlier fieldwork in Seine Bight, and it is concerned primarily with grammatical issues resulting from the contact of Belizean Kriol and Garifuna. In the course of the article Escure remarks that it was difficult to find native speakers of Garifuna under fifty years of age and that the language was in steep decline. However, this particular topic is not the focus of that article, and so it is not investigated there in a formal way.

13. The extent of Ravindranath's (2009: 28) work in Belize is a brief teacher survey conducted one day in the primary school in Seine Bight. According to this study, Seine Bight teachers reported that 80 percent of their students aged eleven to twelve speak Garifuna. Ravindranath's survey was conducted in 2008; so, eight years later, these students would be nineteen to twenty. Of our participants in that age, approximately 31 percent admitted being able to speak Garifuna even a little bit, which is substantially less than what Ravindranath found eight years earlier.

14. This variation by gender seems to follow patterns found in numerous other times and places in which women orient more directly toward standard or prestige forms, while men frequently express greater preference for traditional or vernacular forms. See, for example, Labov 1963, 2001; Trudgill 1972; Wolfram 2008; Eckert 2008; and Salmon 2015.

15. See Creber and Giles 1989; Escure 2004; and Salmon and Gómez Menjívar 2017. See especially Garrett 2010; Soukup 2013; and the sources therein.

16. The events we observed were all very public, everyday occurrences. The goal of our observations was merely to listen for which languages were being spoken, and in most situations no contact whatsoever was made with those we observed. As such, we see no potential areas for ethical concerns to be raised.

17. Here is E. Roy Cayetano (1974) describing an essential part of the Garifuna religion: "The main idea underlying Garifuna religion and perhaps their view of the world is that the spirits of the departed ancestors mediate between the individual and the external world. If the individual performs as he should, then all will be well with him. If not, then the harmony that one desires in his relationship with others and the rest of the external world will

be disrupted. This disruption takes the form of persistent and recurring misfortune or illness that cannot be cured by ordinary known medical practices. This religious or cosmological system implies that the living Garifuna and the ancestral dead have certain responsibilities and obligations to each other. It behooves the living not to neglect the ancestors." For lengthy studies of Garifuna religious practices, see also González 1988; and Kerns 1997.

18. Indeed, the Facebook page of one prominent Seine Bight family, which is dedicated to the family's annual *dugu*, provides detailed instructions for acquiring the proper clothing, learning the proper songs, and so on, as well as extensive lists of supplies needed for holding the event. There are also links to GoFundMe pages inviting contributions and advertisements for various other types of pre-*dugu* fundraisers, including fish fries and barbecue dinners.

19. For extensive discussion of the relation of "usefulness" and language endangerment, see Mufwene 2003. See also the discussion of Mopan in chapter 3, above.

20. It is telling too that, according to González (1988: 91), the Catholic Church "no longer forbids its members to participate in a *dugu*."

CONCLUSION

1. For in-depth discussion of the concept of "language ecology" in the context of language change and shift, see also Mufwene 2001 and 2007.

2. See, for example, Escure 2004 and Ravindranath 2009 on contact-induced change involving Garifuna and Kriol; Balam 2014, 2015, 2016a, and 2016b on Belizean Spanish and Kriol; Chappell (in press) on language attitudes toward Miskitu and Spanish in Bluefields, Nicaragua; and López Alonzo 2014 and 2016 on contact between Creole, Miskito, and Spanish in Bluefields.

3. The face and place of Catholicism changed in the 1830s, as Garifuna communities arrived in the colony as practitioners of a syncretic religion consisting of blended ancestral and Catholic rites after having been catechized in St. Vincent before their deportation to Roatán. The subsequent arrival of thousands of Maya refugees, who were largely practicing Catholics, from the Yucatán Caste War to northern areas of British Honduras accelerated the Church's sponsorship of Jesuit missions to the colony. This religious venture would lead to the founding of the first modern Catholic church in 1851 and many educational institutions, including St. John's High School in 1887 (see Educational Institutions, above).

4. The last three decades have led to an increasing role in adolescents' lives, especially in urban areas, while parents and grandparents are much

less likely to use technology. The teenagers who use it "consider the Internet an excellent resource for learning, entertainment, and expanding social networks," turning this "global space to 'hang out' [into a one that] impacts language usage, music tastes, and other topics adolescents report thinking and talking about" (Anderson-Fye 2007: 85).

5. Representations of the tropics have ranged from paradise to inferno, capturing the dynamics of (linguistic) encounters and confrontations that have underpinned writings about the Caribbean since Columbus announced his "discovery" of Hispaniola in his first letter to the king and queen of Castile, in 1493. For two particularly arresting accounts of such representations, see Rodríguez 2004; and Sá 2004.

6. New archaeological discoveries are still being made in Belize. As recently as 2013, a team of researchers reported on Hats Kaab, a group of structures that may have been used in ceremonies to commemorate astronomical events. The land surrounding the structures had experienced intense forest and clearing of vegetation to make way for rice production, thus greatly impacting the preservation of the "archaeological record" in the area. As recently as 2001, the area had been relatively undisturbed, "shrouded in dense scrub vegetation" much like that of its surroundings (Runggaldier, Brouwer Burg, and Harrison-Buck 2013: 9). As ecotourism and large-scale agricultural production for export advances into the Maya Mountains, we might anticipate further adverse impact on the archaeological and linguistic ecology of this rich mountain range.

Works Cited

Academia de Lenguas Mayas de Guatemala (ALMG). *Tojkinb'eeb' t'an mopan: Gramática descriptiva mopan.* Guatemala City: ALMG, 2001.

———. *Muuch't'an mopan: Vocabulario mopan.* Guatemala City: ALMG, 2003.

———. *Tojkinb'eeb' tz'iib' t'an mopan.* Guatemala City: ALMG, 2004.

Aguirre, Gerardo. *La cruz de Nimajuyú: Historia de la parroquia de San Pedro la Laguna.* Guatemala: Iglesia Católica, 1972.

Aikhenvald, Alexandra. "The Arawak Language Family." In *The Amazonian Languages,* edited by R. M. W. Dixon and Alexandra Aikhenvald, 65–106. Cambridge: Cambridge University Press, 1999.

Albarracín, Lelia Inés. "Lenguas en contacto: Quechua y español en el Noroeste Argentino." Paper presented at the Indigenous Languages and Cultures of Latin America Symposium, Columbus, Ohio, October 2016.

Anderson-Fye, Eileen. "Never Leave Yourself: Ethnopsychology as a Mediator of Psychological Globalization among Belizean Schoolgirls." *Ethos* 31 (2003): 59–94.

———. "Belize." In *International Encyclopedia of Adolescence,* edited by Jeffrey Jensen Arnett, 77–86. New York: Taylor & Francis, 2007.

Archive of the Indigenous Languages of Latin America (AILLA). "The Indigenous Languages of Latin America." http://www.ailla.utexas.org /site/lg_about.html. Accessed May 1, 2016.

Arnove, Robert F., and Carlos J. Ovando. "Contested Ideological, Linguistic and Pedagogical Values in Nicaragua: The Case of the Atlantic Coast." *Bilingual Research Journal* 17, no. 3–4 (1993): 135–61.

Bakhtin, Mikhail. *Speech Genres and Other Late Essays.* Translated by Vern W. McGee. Edited by Caryl Emerson and Michael Holquist. Austin: University of Texas Press, 1950.

Balam, Osmer. "Overt Language Attitudes and Linguistic Identities among Multilingual Speakers in Northern Belize." *Studies in Hispanic and Lusophone Linguistics* 6, no. 2 (2013): 247–77.

———. "Notes on the History and Morphosyntactic Characteristics of Spanish in Northern Belize." *Kansas Working Papers in Linguistics* 35 (2014): 79–94.

———. "Code-Switching and Linguistic Evolution: The Case of 'Hacer + V' in Orange Walk, Northern Belize." *Lengua y Migración* 7, no. 1 (2015): 83–109.

————. "Semantic Categories and Gender Assignment in Contact Spanish: Type of Code-Switching and its Relevance to Linguistic Outcomes." *Journal of Language Contact* 9, no. 3 (2016a): 405-35.

————. "Mixed Verbs in Contact Spanish: Patterns of Use among Emergent and Dynamic Bi/Multilinguals." *Languages* 1, no. 1 (2016b): 3. doi:10.3390/languages1010003.

Balam, Osmer, and Ana de Prada Pérez. "Attitudes towards Spanish and Code-Switching in Belize: Stigmatization and Innovation in the Spanish Classroom." *Journal of Language, Identity and Education* 16 (2017): 17-31.

Balam, Osmer, Ana de Prada Pérez, and Dámaris Mayans. "A Congruence Approach to the Study of Bilingual Compound Verbs in Northern Belize Contact Spanish." *Spanish in Context* 11, no. 2 (2014): 243-65.

Becker Richards, Julia, and Michael Richards. "Mayan Language Literacy in Guatemala: A Socio-historical Overview." In *Indigenous Literacies in the Americas: Language Planning from the Bottom Up*, edited by Nancy H. Hornberger, 189-212. Berlin: Mouton de Gruyter, 1997.

Bolland, Nigel O. *Colonialism and Resistance in Belize: Essays in Historical Sociology*. Benque Viejo del Carmen, Belize: Cubola, 1988.

Bolland, Nigel, and Mark Moberg. "Development and National Identity: Creolization, Immigration and Ethnic Conflict in Belize." *International Journal of Comparative Race and Ethnic Studies* 2 (1995): 1-18.

Bonner, Donna. "Garifuna Children's Language Shame: Ethnic Stereotypes, National Affiliation, and Transnational Immigration as Factors in Language Choice in Southern Belize." *Language in Society* 30 (2001): 81-96.

Breton, Raymond. *Dictionaire caraibe-françois, meslé de quantité de remarques historiques pour l'esclaircissement de la langue. Composé par le R.P. Raymond Breton, Religieux de l'ordre des Freres Prescheurs, et l'un des premiers Missionnaires Apostoliques en l'isle de la Gardeloupe et autres circonvoisines de l'Amerique.* Auxerre: Gilles Bouquet, imprimeur ordinaire du ROY, 1665.

Cabrera, Luis. "The Key to the Mexican Chaos." In *Renascent Mexico*, edited by Hubert Herring and Herbert Weinstock, 11-29. New York: Covici Freide, 1935.

Cámara de Diputados (Mexico). "Ley general de derechos lingüísticos de los pueblos indígenas: Última reforma." *Diario Oficial de la Federación*, December 17, 2015. http://www.diputados.gob.mx/LeyesBiblio/pdf/257_171215.pdf.

Campbell, Lyle. *American Indian Languages: The Historical Linguistics of Native America*. Oxford: Oxford University Press, 1997.

Cardona Fuentes, Pedro David. "Oralidad y documentación lingüística:

Notas sobre el corpus oral del zapoteco del istmo en San Blas Atempa." Paper presented at the Indigenous Languages and Cultures of Latin America Symposium, Columbus, Ohio, October 2016.

Castellanos, Bianet. *A Return to Servitude: Maya Migration and the Tourist Trade in Cancún*. Minneapolis: University of Minnesota Press, 2010.

Castillo, Isidro. *México y su revolución educativa*. Mexico City: Academia Mexicana de la Educación, 1965.

Cayetano, E. Roy. "Song and Ritual as a Key to Understanding Garifuna Personality." Fall 1974. http://ngcbelize.org/the-culture/53-2/song-and -rituals/.

Chappell, Whitney. "Las ideologías lingüísticas de los miskitus hacia la lengua indígena (el miskitu) y la lengua mayoritaria (el español)." *Hispanic Studies Review* (in press).

Choi, Jinny. "[-Person] Direct Object Drop: The Genetic Cause of a Syntactic Feature in Paraguayan Spanish." *Hispania* 83 (2000): 531-43.

Cifuentes, Barbara, and José Luis Moctezuma. "The Mexican Indigenous Languages and the National Censuses: 1970-2000." In *Mexican Indigenous Languages at the Dawn of the Twenty-First Century*, edited by Margarita Hidalgo, 191-248. Berlin: Mouton de Gruyter, 2006.

Congreso de la República de Guatemala. "Decreto Número 19-2003." 2003. https://www.unicef.org/guatemala/spanish/LeyIdiomasNacionales.pdf.

Constitute Project. "Nicaragua 1987 (Revised 2014)." https://www.constitute project.org/constitution/Nicaragua_2014?lang=en. Accessed October 20, 2016.

———. "Paraguay 1992 (Revised 2011)." https://www.constituteproject.org /constitution/Paraguay_2011?lang=en. Accessed October 20, 2016.

Creber, Clare, and Howard Giles. "Social Context and Language Attitudes: The Role of Formality-Informality of the Setting." *Language Sciences* 5 (1989): 155-62.

Danziger, Eve. "Split Intransitivity and Active-Inactive Patterning in Mopan Maya." *International Journal of American Linguistics* 62, no. 4 (1996): 379-414.

———. *Relatively Speaking: Language, Thought, and Kinship among the Mopan Maya*. New York: Oxford University Press, 2001.

Davis, Roy. *Anansi Party: Belizean Folktales and Poems*. Belize City: Factory, 2004.

de Alvarado, Pedro. *An Account of the Conquest of Guatemala in 1524 by Pedro de Alvarado*. Translated by Sedley J. Mackie. New York: Cortes Society, 1924.

Decker, Ken. *The Song of Kriol: A Grammar of the Kriol Language of Belize*. Belmopan, Belize: National Kriol Council, House of Culture, 2005.

Dennis, Philip A. "The Costeños and the Revolution in Guatemala." *Journal of Interamerican Studies and World Affairs* 23, no. 3 (1981): 271–96.

do Couto, Hildo Honório. *Ecolingüística: Estudo das relações entre língua e meio ambiente.* Brasilia: Thesaurus, 2007.

———. "Amerindian Language Islands in Brazil." In *Iberian Imperialism and Language Evolution in Latin America,* edited by Salikoko S. Mufwene, 76–107. Chicago: University of Chicago Press, 2014.

Dorian, Nancy. "Minority and Endangered Languages." In *The Handbook of Bilingualism,* edited by Tej K. Bhatia and William C. Ritchie, 437–59. Malden, Mass.: Blackwell, 2004.

Duncan, Quince. *Cuentos de Hermano Araña.* San José, Costa Rica: Nueva Década, 1991.

Eckert, Penelope. "Variation and the Indexical Field." *Journal of Sociolinguistics* 12 (2008): 453–76.

Edwards, Joyce Anglin. *Anancy in Limón.* San José, Costa Rica: Editorial Costa Rica, 2002.

Ergood, Bruce. "Can Nationalism Survive the Ethnic Revival? The Belizean Situation." In *Belize: Selected Proceedings from the Second Interdisciplinary Conference,* edited by Michael Phillips, 155–71. Lanham, Md.: University Press of America, 1996.

Escure, Geneviève. "Decreolization in a Creole Continuum: Belize." In *Historicity and Variation in Creole Studies,* edited by Arnold Highfield and Albert Valdman, 27–49. Ann Arbor, Mich.: Karoma, 1981.

———. "Gender Roles and Linguistic Variation in the Belizean Creole Community." In *English around the World,* edited by Jenny Cheshire, 595–608. Cambridge: Cambridge University Press, 1991.

———. *Creole and Dialect Continua.* Amsterdam: John Benjamins, 1997.

———. "Garifuna in Belize and Honduras." In *Creoles, Contact, and Language Change: Linguistic and Social Implications,* edited by Geneviève Escure and Armin Schwegler, 35–65. Amsterdam: Benjamins, 2004.

———. "Pidgins/Creoles and Discourse." In *The Handbook of Pidgin and Creole Studies,* edited by Silvia Kouwenberg and John Victor Singler, 567–92. Malden, Mass.: Blackwell, 2008.

Ethnologue: Languages of the World. 20th ed. Dallas: SIL International, 2017a. http://www.ethnologue.com.

Ethnologue: Languages of the World. "Guaraní, Paraguayan." 2017b. https://www.ethnologue.com/language/gug.

Ethnologue: Languages of the World. "Mískito." 2017c. https://www.ethnologue.com/language/miq.

Ethnologue: Languages of the World. "Nicaragua Creole English." 2017d.
https://www.ethnologue.com/language/bzk.

Ferguson, Charles. "Diglossia." In *Language in Culture and Society*, edited
by Dell Hymes, 429–39. New York: Harper and Row, 1959.

Fishman, Joshua. *Sociolinguistics: A Brief Introduction.* Rowley: Newbury,
1970.

———. *Reversing Language Shift: Theoretical and Empirical Foundations of
Assistance to Threatened Languages.* Bristol, U.K.: Multilingual Matters,
1991.

———. "Language Maintenance, Language Shift, and Reversing Language
Shift." In *The Handbook of Bilingualism*, edited by Tej K. Bhatia and
William C. Ritchie, 406–36. Malden, Mass.: Blackwell, 2004.

Fishman, Joshua, and Ofelia García. *Handbook of Language and Ethnic
Identity.* New York: Oxford University Press, 2010.

Freeland, Jane. "Gaining and Realizing Language Rights in a Multilingual
Region." In *National Integration and Contested Autonomy: The
Caribbean Coast of Nicaragua*, edited by Luciano Baracco, 243–82.
New York: Algora, 2011.

García, Ofelia, Dina López, and Carmina Makar. "Latin America." *Handbook
of Language and Ethnic Identity*, edited by Joshua Fishman and Ofelia
García, 353–73. Oxford: Oxford University Press, 2010.

Garrett, Peter. *Attitudes to Language.* Cambridge: Cambridge University
Press, 2010.

Gómez Menjívar, Jennifer Carolina. "Liminal Citizenry: Black Experience
in the Central American Intellectual Imagination." PhD diss., Ohio State
University, 2011.

Gómez Menjívar, Jennifer Carolina, and William Salmon. "Attitudes and
Endangerment in a Mopan Community." *Chicago Linguistic Society*
52 (forthcoming).

González, Nancie. *Sojourners of the Caribbean: Ethnogenesis and
Ethnohistory of the Garifuna.* Urbana: University of Illinois Press, 1988.

Granadillo, Tania. "El 'Gloria al Bravo Pueblo' en tres lenguas indígenas:
Contexto socio-político y estrategias lingüísticas." Paper presented at
the Indigenous Languages and Cultures of Latin America Symposium,
Columbus, Ohio, October 2016.

Greene, Laurie. *A Grammar of Belizean Creole.* New York: Peter Lang, 1999.

Gregory, James R. "Pioneers on a Cultural Frontier: The Mopan Maya of
British Honduras." PhD diss., University of Pittsburgh, 1972.

———. "The Modification of the Inter-ethnic Boundary in Belize."
American Ethnologist 3, no. 4 (1976): 683–708.

Gynan, Shaw. "Language Policy and Planning in Paraguay." In *Language Planning and Policy in Latin America: Ecuador, Mexico and Paraguay*, edited by Richard B. Baldauf and Robert B. Kaplan, 218–83. Clevdon: Multilingual Matters, 2007.

Haboud, Marleen. "Investigación interdisciplinaria: Por el reencuentro con las lenguas ancestrales del Ecuador y el empoderamiento de sus hablantes." Paper presented at the Indigenous Languages and Cultures of Latin America Symposium, Columbus, Ohio, October 2016.

Hagerty, Timothy W. "The Influence of English on the Spanish of Belize." In *Belize: Selected Proceedings from the Second Interdisciplinary Conference*, edited by Michael Phillips, 131–42. Lanham, Md.: University Press of America, 1996.

Hale, Charles. *Resistance and Contradiction: Miskitu Indians and the Nicaraguan State, 1894–1987*. Stanford, Calif.: Stanford University Press, 1994.

Haugen, Einar. *The Ecology of Language*. Stanford, Calif.: Stanford University Press, 1972.

Heath, Shirley Brice. *La política del lenguaje en México: De la colonia a la nación*. Mexico City: Instituto Nacional Indigenista, 1972.

Helms, Mary W. "Matrilocality and the Maintenance of Ethnic Identity: The Miskito of Eastern Nicaragua and Honduras." Paper presented at Verhandlungen des achtunddrei-bigsten internationalen Amerikanisten Kongresses, Stuttgart, Germany, 1968.

———. "The Cultural Ecology of a Colonial Tribe." *Ethnology* 8, no. 1 (1969): 76–84.

Hernández Arana Xajilá, Francisco. *Anales de los cakchiqueles/Annals of the Caqchiquels* [1507]. Translated by Adrian Recinos and Adriana Goetz. Norman: University of Oklahoma Press, 1953.

Hernández Cervantes, Alfonso. "Enseñanza-aprendizaje del náwatl en la universidad: Materiales didácticos." Paper presented at the Indigenous Languages and Cultures of Latin America Symposium, Columbus, Ohio, October 2016.

Herrera, Yvette, Myrna Manzanares, Silvaana Udz, Cynthia Crosbie, and Ken Decker. *Kriol-Inglish Dikshineri/English-Kriol Dictionary*. Belmopan, Belize: National Kriol Council, House of Culture, 2010.

Hidalgo, Margarita. "Sociolinguistic Stratification in New Spain." *International Journal of the Sociology of Language* 149 (2001): 55–78.

Hidalgo, Margarita, ed. *Mexican Indigenous Languages at the Dawn of the Twenty-First Century*. Berlin: Mouton de Gruyter, 2006.

Hofling, Charles A. *Mopan Maya-Spanish-English Dictionary*. Salt Lake City: University of Utah Press, 2011.

Holm, John. "Miskito Words in Belizean Creole." *Belizean Studies* 5 (1977): 1–19.

———. *Central American English*. Amsterdam: John Benjamins, 1983.

Institute for Social and Cultural Research (ISCR). "The National Garifuna Council: Its Achievements." N.d. http://www.nichbelize.org/iscr -featured-organization/the-national-garifuna-council-its-achievements .html.

Johnson, Melissa. "The Making of Race and Place in 19th-Century British Honduras," *Environmental History* 8 (2003): 598–617.

Jones, Grant D. *Maya Resistance to Spanish Rule: Time and History on a Colonial Frontier*. Albuquerque: University of New Mexico Press, 1989.

Julca Guerrero, Felix Claudio. "Linguistic and Sociolinguistic Views of Andean Hypocorisms." Paper presented at the Indigenous Languages and Cultures of Latin America Symposium, Columbus, Ohio, October 2016.

Kaufman, Terrance, and John S. Justeson. *A Preliminary Mayan Etymological Dictionary*, October 2003. http://www.famsi.org/reports /01051/pmed.pdf. Accessed January 2016.

Kerns, Virginia. *Women and the Ancestors: Black Carib Kinship and Ritual*. Urbana: University of Illinois Press, 1997.

Key, Carol. "Cayes, Coral, Tourism, and Ethnicity in Belize." PhD diss., University of North Texas, 2002.

Klee, Carol, and Andrew Lynch. *El español en contacto con otras lenguas*. Washington, D.C.: Georgetown University Press, 2009.

Kristiansen, Tore. "Attitudes, Ideology, and Awareness." In *The SAGE Handbook of Sociolinguistics*, edited by Ruth Wodak, Barbara Johnstone, and Paul E. Kerswill, 265–78. Los Angeles: SAGE, 2011.

Labov, William. "The Social Motivation of a Sound Change." *Word* 19 (1963): 273–309.

———. *Sociolinguistic Patterns*. Philadelphia: University of Pennsylvania Press, 1972.

———. *Principles of Linguistic Change*, vol. 2, *Social Factors*. Malden, Mass.: Wiley-Blackwell, 2001.

Le Page, Robert. "You Can Never Tell Where a Word Comes From: Language Contact in a Diffuse Setting." In *Language Contact: Theoretical and Empirical Studies*, edited by Ernst Jahr, 70–101. The Hague: Mouton, 1992.

Le Page, Robert, and Andrée Tabouret-Keller. *Acts of Identity: Creole-Based Approaches to Language and Ethnicity*. Cambridge: Cambridge University Press, 1985.

López Alonzo, Karen. "El estatus del español en Bluefields, Nicaragua." Lecture, University of Minnesota Duluth, November 11, 2014.

————. "Rhotic Production in the Spanish of Bluefields, Nicaragua: A Language Contact Situation." PhD diss., The Ohio State University, 2016.

Lutz, Christopher. "Santiago de Guatemala, 1541–1773: The Sociodemographic History of a Spanish-American Colonial City." PhD diss., University of Wisconsin, Madison, 1976.

McClaurin, Irma. *Women of Belize: Gender and Change in Central America.* New Brunswick: Rutgers University Press, 1996.

McKenna Brown, R. "A Brief Cultural History of the Guatemalan Highlands." In *The Life of Our Language: Kaqchikel Maya Maintenance, Shift, and Revitalization*, edited by Susan Garzon, R. McKenna Brown, Julia Becker Richards and Wuqu' Ajpub', 44–61. Austin: University of Texas Press, 1998.

Ministry of Education. *2008 Belize National Standards and Curriculum Web for Language Arts.* http://moe.gov.bz/rubberdoc/71d37e055d0ce2babc38 7f5f908beeff.pdf. 2008. Accessed July 2012.

Moberg, Mark. *Myths of Ethnicity and Nation: Immigration, Work and Identity in the Belize Banana Industry.* Knoxville: University of Tennessee Press, 1997.

Montrul, Silvina. *El bilingüismo en el mundo hispanoamericano.* Hoboken, N.J.: Wiley-Blackwell, 2012.

Morales-Good, Monica. "La alfabetización de los pueblos indígenas mexicanos: Todo no es suficiente." Paper presented at the Indigenous Languages and Cultures of Latin America Symposium, Columbus, Ohio, October 2016.

Mosby, Dorothy. *Place, Language and Identity in Afro-Costa Rican Literature.* Columbia: University of Missouri Press, 2003.

Mufwene, Salikoko. *The Ecology of Language Evolution.* Cambridge: Cambridge University Press, 2001.

————. "What Have Pride and Prestige Got to Do with It?" In *When Languages Collide*, edited by Brian D. Joseph, 324–46. Columbus: Ohio State University Press, 2003.

————. "How Languages Die." In *Combat pour les langues du monde/ Fighting for the World's Languages: Hommage à Claude Hagège*, edited by Jocelyne Fernández-Vest, 377–88. Paris: L'Harmattan, 2006.

————. "Population Movements and Contacts: Competition, Selection, and Language Evolution." *Journal of Language Contact* 1 (2007): 63–91.

Mufwene, Salikoko, ed. *Iberian Imperialism and Language Evolution in Latin America.* Chicago: University of Chicago Press, 2014.

Murnane, Richard, John Mullens, and John Willett. "The Contribution of Training and Subject Matter Knowledge to Teaching Effectiveness: A

Multi-level Analysis of Longitudinal Evidence from Belize." *Comparative Education Review* 40, no. 2 (1996): 139–57.

Murray, Mariel. "As Ye Sow, Ye Shall Reap: Granting Maya Women Land Rights to Gain Maya Land Rights." *William and Mary Journal of Women and Law* 18, no. 3 (2012): 651–87.

Muyolema, Armando. "Revitalización, oralidad y pedagogía de las lenguas minoritarias." Paper presented at the Indigenous Languages and Cultures of Latin America Symposium, Columbus, Ohio, October 2016.

Nembhard, Jessica. *The Nation We Are Making: A Junior History of Belize.* Belize City: Ministry of Education, 1990.

Nettle, Daniel, and Suzanne Romaine. *Vanishing Voices: The Extinction of the World's Languages.* Oxford: Oxford University Press, 2000.

Oland, Maxine Heather. "Long-Term Indigenous History on a Colonial Frontier: Archaeology at a 15th–17th Century Maya Village, Progresso Lagoon, Belize." PhD diss., Northwestern University, 2009.

Palacio, Joseph. "Food and Social Relations in a Garifuna Village." PhD diss., University of California, Berkeley, 1982.

———. *The Garifuna: A Nation across Borders.* Benque Viejo del Carmen, Belize: Cubola, 2005.

Parodi, Claudia. "The Indianization of Spaniards in New Spain." In *Mexican Indigenous Languages at the Dawn of the Twenty-First Century*, edited by Margarita Hidalgo, 29–52. Berlin: Mouton de Gruyter, 2006.

Pineda, Baron L. *Shipwrecked Identities: Navigating Race on Nicaragua's Mosquito Coast.* New Brunswick, N.J.: Rutgers University Press, 2006.

Ramclan, Adler, and Kirkland Smith. *Anansi ton wahn oal man.* Belize City: Belize Kriol Project, 2004.

Ravindranath, Maya. "Language Shift and the Speech Community: Sociolinguistic Change in a Garifuna Community in Belize." PhD diss., University of Pennsylvania, 2009.

Reisman, Karl. "Cultural and Linguistic Ambiguity in a West Indian Village." In *Afro-American Anthropology: Contemporary Perspectives*, edited by Norman Whitten and John Szwed, 129–44. New York: Free Press, 1970.

Rickford, John. "Standard and Non-standard Language Attitudes in a Creole Continuum." In *Language of Inequality*, edited by Nessa Wolfson and Joan Manes, 145–60. The Hague: Mouton, 1985.

———. "Sociolinguistic Variation in Cane Walk." In *English around the World*, edited by Jenny Cheshire, 609–18. Cambridge: Cambridge University Press, 1991.

Robinson, St. John. "The Chinese of Central America: Diverse Beginnings, Common Achievements." *Journal of Chinese Overseas* 5, no. 1 (2009): 91–114.

Rodríguez, Ileana. *Transatlantic Topographies: Islands, Highlands and Jungles*. Minneapolis: University of Minnesota Press, 2004.

Romero, Simon. "An Indigenous Language with Unique Staying Power." *New York Times*, March 12, 2012. http://www.nytimes.com/2012/03/12/world/americas/in-paraguay-indigenous-language-with-unique-staying-power.html.

Rosales Caro, César Felipe. "Balanced Bilingualism Pewenche: Spanish in the Alto Bío Pewenche Community." Paper presented at the Indigenous Languages and Cultures of Latin America Symposium, Columbus, Ohio, October 2016.

Rosenberg, Peter. Vergleichende Sprachinselforschung: Sprachwandel in deutschen Sprachinseln in Russland und Brasilien. *Linguistik online* 13, nos. 1–3: 273–323.

Rubin, Joan. *Bilingüismo nacional en Paraguay*. Mexico City: Instituto Indigenista Interamericano, 1974.

Rubio, Paul. "Francis Ford Coppola's Belize Beauties." *Ocean Home: The Luxury Coastal Lifestyle Magazine*, June–July 2012. http://www.ocean homemag.com/April-May-2012/Francis-Ford-Coppolas-Belize-Beauties/.

Ruiz Puga, Davida Nicolás. "Panorama del texto literario en Belice, de tiempos coloniales a tiempos post-coloniales." *Istmo: Revista de Estudios Culturales Centroamericanos* 1 (2001): 1–4. http://istmo.denison.edu/n01/articulos/panorama.html.

Runggaldier, Astrid, Marieka Brouwer Burg, and Eleanor Harrison-Buck. "Hats Kaab: A Newly Discovered E-group at the Closing of the 13th Baktun." *Research Reports in Belizean Archaeology* 10 (2013): 65–75.

Sá, Lucia. *Rain Forest Literatures: Amazonian Texts and Latin American Culture*. Minneapolis: University of Minnesota Press, 2004.

Salmon, William. "The Contrastive Discourse Marker *ata* in Belizean Kriol." *Lingua* 143 (2014): 86–102.

———. "Language Ideology, Gender, and Varieties of Belizean Kriol." *Journal of Black Studies* 46 (2015): 1–21.

———. "Irrealis and Emphatic: A Corpus Study of the *Bee* Copula in Belizean Kriol." *English World-Wide* 37, no. 3 (2016): 323–49.

Salmon, William, and Jennifer Gómez Menjívar. "Whose Kriol Is Moa Beta? Prestige and Dialects of Kriol in Belize." *Berkeley Linguistics Society* 40 (2014): 456–79.

———. "Language Variation and Dimensions of Prestige in Belizean Kriol." *Journal of Pidgin and Creole Languages* 31, no. 2 (2016): 316–60.

———. "Setting and Language Attitudes in a Creole Context." *Applied Linguistics* (2017). doi: https://doi.org/10.1093/applin/amx017.

Sankoff, Gillian. "Linguistic Outcomes of Language Contact." In *Handbook of Sociolinguistics*, edited by Peter Trudgill, J. K. Chambers, and Natalie Schilling-Estes, 638–68. Oxford, U.K.: Blackwell, 2004.

Sapper, Karl T. *Das nordliche Mittel-Amerika nebst einem Ausflug nach dem Hochland von Anahuac: Reisen und Studien aus den Jahren 1888–1895.* Braunschweig, Germany: Friederich Vieweg und Sohn, 1897.

Shoman, Assad. *A History of Belize in 13 Chapters.* Belize City: Angelus, 2011.

Smart, Ian. *Central American Writers of West Indian Origin: A New Hispanic Literature.* Washington, D.C.: Three Continents, 1984.

Soukup, Barbara. "The Measurement of 'Language Attitudes'— A Reappraisal from a Constructionist Perspective." In *Language (De)standardization in Late Modern Europe: Experimental Studies*, edited by Tore Kristiansen and Stefan Grondelaers, 251–66. Oslo: Novus, 2013.

Spykman, Nicholas John. *The Geography of the Peace.* San Diego: Harcourt Brace, 1944.

Statistical Institute of Belize. *2010 Belize Population and Housing Census Report.* http://www.statisticsbelize.org.bz/dms2ouc/dynamicdata/docs/20110505004542_2.pdf. Accessed July 1, 2013.

Steinberg, Michael K. "Tourism Development and Indigenous People: The Maya Experience in Southern Belize." *Focus* 44, no. 2 (1994): 17–20.

Straughan, Jerome. "Emigration from Belize since 1981." In *Taking Stock: Belize at 25 Years of Independence*, edited by Barbara Susan Balboni and Joseph O. Palacio, 254–79. Benque Viejo del Carmen, Belize: Cubola, 2007.

Sutherland, Anne. *The Making of Belize: Globalization in the Margins.* Westport, Conn.: Greenwood, 1998.

Sutton, Constance. "Afterword." *Women and the Ancestors: Black Carib Kinship and Ritual.* Urbana: University of Illinois Press, 1997.

Tanaka, Yuki. "Exploring a Heritage Language: Linguistic Ideologies, Identity and Revitalization of Belizean Mopan." Paper presented at Symposium on Teaching and Learning Indigenous Languages of Latin America, October 30–November 2, 2011. Proceedings published July 2012. https://kellogg.nd.edu/STLILLA/proceedings/Tanaka_Yuki.pdf.

Tanaka-McFarlane, Yuki. "Re-examining the Role of Language Documentation as a Medium in Relation to Language Renewal Efforts, 'Purity' Ideologies and Affects among Belizean Mopan Speakers. *Texas Linguistics Forum* 58 (2015): 139–51.

Taylor, Douglas. *The Black Carib of British Honduras.* New York: Wenner-Gren Foundation, 1951.

Thomason, Sarah. "Language Change and Language Contact." In

Encyclopedia of Language and Linguistics, edited by Keith Brown, 339-46. Oxford, U.K.: Elsevier, 2006.

———. "Contact Explanations in Linguistics." In *The Handbook of Language Contact,* edited by Raymond Hickey, 31-47. Oxford, U.K.: Blackwell, 2010.

Thompson, J. Eric S. *Ethnology of the Mayas of Southern and Central British Honduras.* Chicago: Field Museum of Natural History, 1930.

Toledo Maya Cultural Council. *Maya Atlas: The Struggle to Preserve Maya Land in Southern Belize.* Berkeley: North Atlantic Books, 1997.

———. "The Toledo Maya Cultural Council." http://geog.berkeley.edu/ProjectsResources/MayanAtlas/MayaAtlas/TMCC.htm#resolve. Accessed September 10, 2017.

Trudgill, Peter. "Sex, Covert Prestige and Linguistic Change in the Urban British English of Norwich." *Language in Society* 1 (1972): 179-95.

Tumul K'in Center of Learning. "Eco-tourism." http://www.tumulkinbelize.org/eco_tourism.html. Accessed March 15, 2017.

Udz, Silvaana. "Improving Kriol Language Attitude and English Accuracy: An Exploratory Study." Paper presented at the 2013 Belize International Symposium on Education, Belize City, January 2013.

University of Belize, Natural Resources Management Program. *Rapid Assessment of Effects and Issues Related to Development in the Placencia Area, Dry Season 2011.* NRMP 4552, Integrated Coastal Zone Management, 2011. http://www.pcsdbelize.org/placencia-assessment.pdf.

Vandekerckhove, Reinhild. "Urban and Rural Language." In *Language and Space: An International Handbook of Linguistic Variation,* edited by Peter Auer and Jürgen Erich Schmidt, 315-32. Berlin: De Gruyter, 2010.

Van Oss, Adriaan. *Catholic Catholicism: A Parish History of Guatemala, 1524-1821.* Cambridge: Cambridge University Press, 1986.

Vargas, Giselle Chang. *Cuentos tradicionales afrolimonenses.* San Jose, Costa Rica: Editorial Costa Rica, 2006.

Vásquez Carranza, Ariel. "Linguistic Rights in Mexico." *Revista Electrónica de Lingüística Aplicada* 8 (2009): 199-210.

Vedovato, Odair. "'Os ossos do irmão dele': Uma narrativa tradicional Laklãnõ recuperada." Paper presented at the Indigenous Languages and Cultures of Latin America Symposium. Columbus, Ohio, October 2016.

von Gleich, Utta, and Wolfgang Wölck. "Changes in Language Use and Attitudes of Quechua-Spanish Bilinguals in Peru." In *Language in the Andes,* edited by Peter Cole, 27-50. Newark: University of Delaware Press, 1994.

———. "Alberto Escobar y la sociolingüística peruana: Una valoración." *Lexis* 24 (2001): 367–79.

Voorhees, Mara, and Joshua Brown. *Lonely Planet: Belize*. Oakland, Calif.: Lonely Planet, 2008.

Wilk, Richard. "Beauty and the Feast: Official and Visceral Nationalism in Belize." *Ethnos* 53 (1993): 1–25.

———. "'Real Belizean Food': Building Local Identity in the Transnational Caribbean." *American Anthropologist* 101 (1999): 244–55.

Wilk, Richard, and Mac Chapin. *Ethnic Minorities in Belize: Mopan, Kekchi, and Garifuna*. Belize City: Society for the Promotion of Education and Research, 1990.

Winford, Donald. "The Caribbean." In *English around the World*, edited by Jenny Cheshire, 565–84. Cambridge: Cambridge University Press, 1991.

Wölck, Wolfgang. "Diglossia, Stable Bilingualism, and Minority Language Maintenance." *International Journal of Anthropology* 23 (2008): 221–32.

Wolfram, Walt. "When Islands Lose Dialects." *Shima: The International Journal of Research into Island Cultures* 2 (2008): 2–13.

World Travel and Tourism Council. *Travel & Tourism: Economic Impact 2017, Belize*. https://www.wttc.org/-/media/files/reports/economic-impact -research/countries-2017/belize2017.pdf. Accessed May 1, 2017.

Young, Colville. "Belize Creole: A Study of the Creolized English Spoken in the City of Belize in Its Cultural and Social Setting." PhD diss., University of York, 1973.

———. *Language and Education in Belize*. Belize City: Angelus, 2002.

Young, Sir William. "Account of the Black Charaibs of St. Vincent with the Charaib Treaty of 1779 and Other Original Documents." In *Journal of a Voyage Undertaken in 1792*. London: n.p., 1795.

Zarratea, Tadeo. "Marco jurídico de las lenguas en Paraguay." Paper presented at the Seminario Nacional de Bilingüismo y Políticas Lingüísticas, Asunción, Paraguay, July 1995.

CPSIA information can be obtained
at www.ICGtesting.com
Printed in the USA
LVOW03s1915250318
1088LV00001B/5/P